BUILDINGS OF EUROPE

BAROQUE EUROPE

With an Introduction by
JAMES LEES-MILNE

Edited by
HARALD BUSCH AND BERND LOHSE

With Commentaries on the Illustrations by
EVA-MARIA WAGNER

Second Edition

THE MACMILLAN COMPANY
NEW YORK

TRANSLATED BY PETER GORGE

FIRST PUBLISHED, 1962

LIBRARY OF CONGRESS CATALOG NUMBER: 62–51825

INTRODUCTION

The very word Baroque—at least in the sense which we attach to it—was unknown to the men who lived in the Baroque age. Barroco, a term for a misshapen pearl discarded on the seashore by Portuguese fishermen, had until the late nineteenth century when Baroque art was totally superannuated and despised only a localized pejorative meaning. Indeed there was no such recognized thing as Baroque art even one hundred years ago. Art historians simply acknowledged that there was a phase—and rather too long a one—of late Renaissance art, much to be deplored on account of its over-exuberant and decadent manifestations.

That the rudimentary physical attributes of Baroque architecture followed the broad lines observed by Renaissance architecture goes without saying. Baroque architecture was like the other based strictly on the classical orders. Only its interpretation of them was different and far more free. It concentrated upon curved and sinuous plans, contrasting contours of surface, flowing forms, dramatic lighting effects and the merging of naturalistic sculpture and realistic painting with the structure. That its dominant essence, like that of Renaissance architecture, had been brought about by a revolutionary process of thought, is not so generally recognized. Whereas Renaissance architecture was the outcome of that revived cult of humanism, believed common to pagan times, Baroque architecture expressed the triumphant recovery of the Catholic Church's deep spiritual values which it had enjoyed in mediaeval times and subsequently lost. To that extent the two styles were fundamentally opposed. We may then well ask how the transition from one to the other happened. Was the change abrupt? The answer to this question is No. Historians have lately concluded that there was first an intervening style which they term Mannerist. It endured from about 1520 to 1570. There was too a second which we shall call Counter-Reformation.

In Italy from about 1570 until 1620 a new, sad Counter-Reformation style succeeded the disruptive Mannerist. A stiff, severe, somewhat inquisitorial expression spread across church façades in the last quarter of the sixteenth century. Della Porta's Gesù front, 1573 (ill. 2) in two stages laced by serried pilasters, the upper crowned with a pedimented centrepiece and flanked by heavy scrolls turned down over the aisles like disapproving lips, became the prototype of church façades all over Europe for several decades. This forbidding and minatory front seemed calculated to keep at bay the would-be transgressor or heretic. Yet it displayed a cohesion of design which was a total departure from Renaissance and Mannerist independence of units. It was a forecast of Baroque wholeness of pattern. A generation later Carlo Maderna added a similar façade to S. Susanna in Rome (1595—1603, ill. 9); and four years after its completion he began the immense front of St. Peter's (ill. 28). Because of the cathedral's infinitely greater scale the front was not of two stages but one. The mobility of the giant columns and of the openings and crestings of the attic is an earnest of that greater rhythm and freedom which were soon to come.

They came in a full-blooded way with Gian Lorenzo Bernini (1598—1680), an outstanding figure in the realm of seventeenth-century art, the high priest of the Baroque movement and one of the greatest sculptors and architects of all time. Bernini's genius would inevitable have asserted itself no matter into what age the man had been born. But let there be no underestimating the fortunate coincidence of his life with a critical phase of the Church's history and a succession of remarkable popes. With the turn of the century the militantly aggressive discipline of the Counter-Reformation was noticeably relaxing. The Reformation was forgotten in the sense that what was lost to the Church of Christ had long been lost and no further encroachments were deemed imminent. The uncompromising doctrines of the Council of Trent which had regulated the Counter-Reformation policy were now largely disregarded. Instead the Church adopted, through the influence of the worldly-wise Jesuits, a new technique of keeping the faithful within the fold by appealing to their love of drama, pageantry and gaiety–always the most successful means of winning the hearts and dominating the souls of simple Latin peoples. Paul V (1605–21), Urban VIII (1623–44), Innocent X (1644–55) and Alexander V (1655–67) had comparatively long reigns. All were men of the highest culture, with a genuine love of the arts and elegant living. Moreover they and their families were extremely rich. They became lavish patrons. No circumstances therefore could have been more propitious for artists. Hence Rome became the cradle of the Baroque movement and the Catholic Faith its inspiration.

The importance of Bernini's contribution to architecture lay in his sculptural handling of masses. The most powerful sculptor after Michelangelo, whom he resembled in titanic personality and intensity of religious devotion, he seemed almost to carve his buildings out of their surroundings in the way he carved his figures out of blocks of marble. Consequently his St. Peter's Colonnade (ill. 26) and S. Andrea al Quirinale (ill. 34) have a three-dimensional quality not found in buildings of ancient or Renaissance times. Bernini's influence endured well into the eighteenth century. The Roman Fuga, Galilei and Carlo Fontana, the Venetian Longhena, the Neapolitan Vanvitelli and the cosmopolitan Juvara looked to him as the unsurpassable master of form. His contemporary Borromini (1599–1667) was a man of no less deep devotion and an architect of no less genius. Indeed his imagination was probably more brilliant in that his works were certainly more daring and challenging than Bernini's. Borromini's churches of S. Carlo Borromeo (ills. 36, 38) and S. Ivo (ills. 40, 41), Rome, with their nervous interplay of contour and infusion of naturalistic detail gleaned from intensive study of Roman imperial architecture and from nature, made a tremendous appeal to his immediate successors. Furthermore Borromini's buildings emphasised verticality, thus re-introducing to architecture a flavour almost Gothic. Architects like the Beneventine Raguzzini, the Piedmontese Guarini and Vittone, and the Sicilian Vaccarini carried these foibles to extreme lengths of eccentricity. Guarini's churches of the Holy Shroud and S. Lorenzo (ills. 37, 39) in Turin are the outcome of the most complicated geometrical exercises. The third important pioneer of the Roman Baroque was Pietro Cortona (1596–1669). He was as notable a painter as an architect. He imparted to his buildings, such as S. Maria della Pace (ill. 35), strong pictorial qualities. By means of convex and concave planes he induced contrasting lights, shadows and perspective effects hitherto experienced only on canvas. The Italian seventeenth-century architects raised in addition to churches vast palaces in which the privileged hierarchy of the Baroque age, both spiritual and lay, might live splendidly and display their art treasures. In Rome papal palaces like the Barberini (ill. 15), Chigi, Pamphili and Odeschalchi were distinguished less by their exteriors, which were simple and monumental, than by their suites of galleries, where walls and ceilings were adorned with colourful trompe-l'œil and sumptuous furnishings (ill. 194). In Genoa palaces for merchant princes arose on an even more colossal scale. Nowhere in Italy however were Baroque palaces more distinctive than those floating edifices launched by Longhena in Venice along the Grand Canal (ill. 42) in three deck-like stages upon cyclopean hulls of rustication.

By 1680 the Spanish Baroque had arrived, and in its turn was to last a hundred years until roughly 1780. The influence of the Roman masters upon this unscholarly style, which developed strong national traits, was curiously lacking. From the hands of José de Churriguera (1665–1723), Narciso de Tomé (author of the bewildering Trasparente, 1721–32, in Toledo Cathedral, ill. 77), Leonardo de Figueroa (San Luis,

Seville, 1699–1730) and Luis de Arévalo (the Cartuja Sacristy, ill. 83, at Granada, 1727–64) the style indulged in frenzies of uncontrolled naturalism never witnessed before or since in post-Renaissance Europe and only parallelled in Mexico (ill. 87) and the colonies of South America (ill. 86).

In Portugal where the Church and the Inquisition were far more tolerant than in Spain the Baroque, no less lavish, was yet gayer. Pilgrimage shrines were made to look like pagan temples approached by terraced stairways (ill. 178) and country villas and gardens abounded (ill. 174). Whereas the native builders interpreted the Baroque with naive exuberance a handful of foreign architects, the German J. F. Ludwig (Chapel of St. John the Baptist in São Roque, Lisbon, 1742–48), the Italian Nasoni (the Assunta, Oporto, c. 1735) and the Frenchman Laprade (Coimbra University, 1717–28) raised buildings which were scholarly, beautiful and oddly enough Portuguese.

In Catholic Bavaria, Austria, Bohemia, Poland and even in Orthodox Russia the full Baroque was retarded until the eighteenth century. In the Germanic countries the appalling devastation of the Thirty Years War and in Austria the presence of the Turks were the cause of restrictions on building. When these were lifted at the end of the seventeenth century there burst forth what is probably the most ambitious, most successful and most appealing architecture of the whole astonishing Baroque movement. Unlike the Baroque of the Iberian peninsula, which was outrageous and untutored, that of central Europe, although intensely complicated, was faultlessly disciplined. At first the seventeenth century saw a number of minor Italian architects like the Zuccalli, Carloni, Petrini and Barelli families at work on most of the important buildings in these countries (ills. 90–91). But in the eighteenth century their place was taken by natives of superior ability, often of distinct genius, such as in Germany Schlüter (ill. 96), Pöppelmann, the Asam brothers and Neumann, and in Austria Fischer von Erlach, L. von Hildebrandt (ill. 95), Prandtauer (ill. 122) and the Dientzenhofer family.

Since Germany alone was divided into some three hundred sovereign states and the princes of the Church were drawn exclusively from the semi-royal and aristocratic classes, palaces and monasteries were hardly distinguishable in size, design or splendour. Thus the layout of a spreading palace like Pommersfelden is no more secular than that of a monastery like Melk (ill. 119). The rococo interior of Neumann's Vierzehnheiligen church (ill. 141) is not a whit more sacred than, say, his kaisersaal in the Würzburg Residenz (ill. 192). In both the plethora of statuary, stucco relief and trompe-l'œil painting is frankly and deliciously profane. If German architects–and Bavarian in particular–exulted in French rococo decoration (of which the Amalienburg spiegelsaal (ill. 204) is the ne plus ultra in this respect), Austrian architects tended more and more towards the cold sobriety of French classicism. One of the greatest of the world's classical architects, J. B. Fischer von Erlach, combined in the Karlskirche, Vienna (ill. 113), a profound understanding of the Roman antique with a sympathy for the patrician suavity and elegance of French academism under Louis XIV.

Indeed in anti-Roman France the Baroque was never more than diluted. Even so it was not applied to churches so much as to private hôtels (ills. 46, 47) and châteaux (ill. 53); to the Palace of Versailles (ills. 48, 49) and the town of Nancy (ill. 214).

If the Baroque barely flourished in France, which was after all a Catholic kingdom, it is hardly surprising that it did not properly integrate with the contemporary architecture of the Protestant Low Countries and Scandinavia. Nevertheless to these outlandish countries it percolated in a variety of pale reflexions. On the tall, vertical façade of J. van Eynde's convent chapel at Averbode (ill. 57) only the surface enrichments can be termed more Baroque than Renaissance. In Stockholm Vingboon's Riddarhuset (ill. 56) is a German and Tessin's Drottningholm Palace (ill. 104) a French variant, each of late seventeenth-century date.

V

In England the version was somehow more individual than cosmopolitan. British Baroque was in fact more pronounced than is generally supposed. Even the strict palladian, Inigo Jones, when confronted with the decoration of the double cube room at Wilton (ill. 54), yielded to a heavy-handed interpretation of the contemporary Roman palace interior. Wren never travelled as far as Italy and his St. Paul's (ill. 29) is admittedly influenced by the Invalides church in Paris (ill. 62); nevertheless his Library at Trinity College, Cambridge (ill. 70), owes not a little to Longhena's Venetian palace fronts, whereas Gibbs' Radcliffe Camera (ill. 231) was frankly modelled upon that architect's S. Maria della Salute at the eastern end of the Grand Canal (ill. 43).

Apart from Wren's several steeples (ill. 68) which evoke a romantic nostalgia for the Gothic (never, incidentally, far from the architect's inspiration) and his unique, almost Guarini-like nave of St. Stephen, Walbrook (ill. 69), most British churches from 1660 to 1760 derive little either in plan or internal composition from the Roman seventeenth-century Baroque. Thomas Archer's are a remarkable exception, and the contours of St. John, Smith Square, London (ill. 227), like many of his architectural units, are borrowed straight from Borromini. Country house architecture is another matter. For here, strangely enough, we often come across exteriors which are more Baroque–by which is meant rhythmical and expressive of movement–than those of the Continent, whereas interiors are usually sedately classical. Vanbrugh's Blenheim Palace with its spreading arms, use of the giant order, curved quadrants, rounded bays and extraordinarily fanciful towers is monumental, romantic and audacious. Several of its apartments are noble, but few indulge in that play of perspective, trompe-l'œil or flowing stucco work which in Italy and the Germanic lands run riot in every palace interior of comparable size and date. Only rarely, as in the Italian-born Verrio's Heaven-Room, c. 1700, at Burghley (ill. 168) do we come upon work of all-embracing illusion. And towards the mid-eighteenth century when English wall and ceiling panels sometimes broke into rococo patterns, as in the great hall at Ragley (ill. 103) and the north hall at Claydon (ill. 208), the architectural background was still kept severely palladian and correct.

James Lees-Milne

The formal elements of Baroque architecture are those of the Renaissance. Yet the same tree has sent forth a second branch. Baroque and Classicism–not to be confused with the Classic Revival–develop simultaneously and, like Renaissance and Late Gothic, at times vie with each other, or again, meet and interpenetrate in their innumerable variations.

The Baroque has a close kinship with the art of Michelangelo, Classicism with Alberti and Palladio. A book on Baroque architecture must trace the development of both movements, and show the impact of each throughout Europe, until the final victory of Classicism, when Baroque dynamism had exhausted itself and its social background was no longer. At Il Gesù Vignola breaks with the Renaissance. The simple cornice (ill. 3), the majestic coupled pilasters and the huge barrel-vaulting create a mood of strength and solidity, a mood reflective both of the crisis and the determination of the Church in the sixteenth century. Painting and plasterwork, added a century later, somewhat detract from the original austerity. Yet the change is deliberate: the High Baroque knew exactly what degree of splendour was needed to adopt this gaunt interior to the changed mood of the times.

Il Gesù was to be the archetype of the Baroque church. For two centuries, the nave with flat side chapels and a dome, unified by the flow of Baroque movement, remain the basic theme.

The façade is the work of Giacomo della Porta (ill. 2), who follows Michelangelo in the use of giant orders. These now become an important device in the subordination of the entire building to a central axis.

S. Susanna (ill. 9), represents a further step forward. Its architect, Carlo Maderna (1556–1639) who, born in the north of Italy, was used to the more open way of building of his native region–employs columns instead of pilasters on the ground floor and hollows the façade with large recesses for statues. The graceful curve of the volutes is like a premonition of the verticalism of the later stages of the Baroque.

In 1604, Maderna is appointed chief architect at St. Peter's. A year later, Paul V. Borghese becomes Pope. It is only now, long after the completion of the eastern portion and the dome, that Michelangelo's plan for a centralised interior is finally abandoned. St. Peter's is given a nave on the model of Il Gesù–albeit on a gigantic scale–barrel-vaulted and flanked with side chapels, retaining Michelangelo's pilaster articulation and his proportions. Maderna's nave and façade were begun 1607 (ill. 28). In the use of columns instead of pilasters on the centre block, the design recalls S. Susanna (ill. 9); giant orders rise through two stories to an enormous height. A tall portico projects slightly from the wide front. Bernini had intended to balance the rather

horizontal effect with turrets above the corners. Though unrealised at St. Peter's, the dome between two towers was to become one of the favourite motifs of the Baroque.

LORENZO BERNINI (1598–1680) was born in Naples. His mother was also Neapolitan, his father, a sculptor and painter, came from Tuscany. When still a child, Bernini was brought to Rome, where he remained for the rest of his life, always busy with important commissions. His earliest outstanding patron was Urban VIII, who appointed the twenty-seven-year-old artist architect to St. Peter's. Already four years earlier, Bernini had begun work on the great baldacchino above the High Altar (ill. 27). He employed the usual medieval scheme. But the tremendous upward surge, that makes the pillars seem contorted by a whirlwind and twists the volutes above into a gigantic crown, is something entirely new.

Bernini's baldacchino is a milestone in the history of the decorative arts. Not merely because it was imitated (ill. 31) everywhere, even in anti-Roman England (ill. 30), or because altars and porticos began sprouting twisted columns in innumerable variety: above all, it brought the sudden realisation that the artist was no longer the slave of matter. His imagination was at last set free. Every kind of individual interpretation was now possible. The first step was made towards the architectural phantasies of the Baroque.

At the peak of his career, in the years between 1656–67, Bernini created the piazza of St. Peter's (ills. 26, 33). The crystal-clear disposition, seemingly so simple, the result of complicated perspective calculations, aimed at giving Maderna's heavy façade lightness and elegance. In the unity of portico, loggia and dome it has become the solemn focal point at the end of the pilgrims' path.

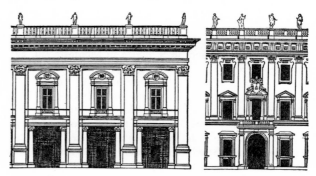

Giant orders appear for the first time in Michelangelo's design of 1564 for the buildings on the Capitol, whose construction was delayed until the seventeenth century (left: Rome, Capitoline Museum). Bernini uses this motif again and again, usually above a simple base (right: Rome, Palazzo Odescalchi, 1665). Later Baroque architects, almost without exception, followed his lead.

VII

Bernini used 284 columns in double rows, open to the west and east. At the eastern end, his colonnades are transformed into closed ambulatories, which, slightly diverging, run towards the raised façade of the church. The eye, at first unable to account for the change in spatial emphasis, only notices the powerful yet harmonious effect of the whole. Façade and dome seem raised on a forest of columns. The figures on the roof line, a procession of Saints, transform the calm of the pillars into flaming upward movement.

Amongst Bernini's other important contributions to the face of Rome are his fountains, none more splendid than the Fontane dei Fiumi on the Piazza Navona (ill. 21), opposite the church of S. Agnese.

On two of his Roman palaces—the Palazzo Chigi-Odescalchi (see drawing) and the Palazzo Montecitorio—the severity of the façade is relieved by a giant order extending through two stories. The slightly projecting bays at the centre at the sides are a first step towards a more three-dimensional architecture. The Palazzo Barberini (ill. 15), begun by Maderna and completed by Bernini 1663, marks the next stage. Arcades and recessed windows have made the façade an elaborate interplay of light and shade. The graceful and open manner of the north, of Palladio and Longhi, has won against the severity and weightiness of Rome.

In the Vatican palace, Bernini solved a most intricate technical problem. The Scala Regia (ill. 25), built between 1663 and 1666, forms the link with St. Peter's. Through the clever use of the Palladian motif of an arch supported on detached columns, a narrow canyon was turned into a marvel of illusionist perspective. Though only the centre passage can be used, the break-up into three has produced startling vistas, and, above all, seemingly greater depth. Towards the top, unknown to the eyes, the columns diminish in size and grow closer. The impression is one of endless continuity.

In hollowing out the piers of the dome of St. Peter's to create niches for altars and statues, Bernini went a long way towards the Baroque transformation of the entire church interior. Scarcely less important to the art of the new epoch are the curving cornices, the broken pediments and the pagan, rather than Christian angels in the dome of the Raimondi chapel in S. Pietro in Montorio (ill. 20) a work of 1636.

At the oblong S. Andrea al Quirinale (ill. 34) Bernini created a façade of the severest simplicity (1668–78). Huge pilasters support an entirely unadorned entablature. The little curved porch provides a most startling contrast. Here is Bernini's mature style, the legacy of the fiery spirit who was the representative p a r e x c e l l e n c e of Rome in the last phase of her glory.

FRANCESCO BORROMINI.

The artist was born in 1599, in the region of Lake Como, not far from the birthplace of his cousin Maderna under whom Borromini was to work as a stonemason at St. Peter's. When Bernini succeeded Maderna in 1629, Borromini stayed on as his assistant. But the two were ill-suited. Borromini, restless and torn by inner conflict, was exactly the opposite of the calm and balanced Bernini. Fame and success, which came to him with his earliest works, brought him no peace. He died from his own hand in 1667.

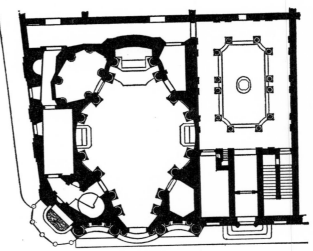

Rome, San Carlo alle quattro Fontane.

His first church, S. Carlo alle quattro Fontane (ill. 36), built between 1638 and 1640, caused a sensation amongst his contemporaries. It is rightly considered 'one of the incunables of the Baroque.' In contrast not only to Bernini's work, but to all tradition, everything is movement. The ground plan consists of two equilateral triangles, which, having the same base, form a rhomboid. The walls billow and recede as if they were modelled rather than made of solid stone. There are no aisles, though between the freestanding columns along the walls, niches open out for statues and side altars. No longer—as in Christian churches from the basilica to the Renaissance—can the beholder discern the mathematical calculations behind the plan. The twice pierced oval dome (ill. 37), thanks to the rapidly foreshortening coffering, appears far taller than it really is. The plan undoubtedly owes some inspiration to the buildings of Imperial Rome. But the general design is entirely Borromini's; its revolutionary significance was understood at once. The façade was not completed until nearly thirty years later. It is Borromini's last work (ill. 38). Curves are everywhere. The orders, detached columns for each storey, are like the framework of a structure whose solids have been almost completely carved away to make room for statues.

At Sant'Ivo alla Sapienza, begun 1642, Borromini reveals another aspect of his revolutionary art (ills. 40, 41). Again, the church is small, hemmed in by buildings, though it does not occupy a corner site like S. Carlo's, but forms the termination of an arcaded courtyard by Giacomo della Porta, the architect of the front of Il Gesù. Borromini's façade, quite unrelated to his interior, fits completely into the existing arrangement. Della Porta's cornice and his rows of pilasters, are continued. Only in the region of the dome, where considerations for the earlier work need no longer count, has Borromini allowed himself some freedom. The drum, strengthened at the joints by pilasters, swells out. The plan similarly breaks with tradition. Based on a six-pointed star, it corresponds in all its compartments to the fantastic outlines of the cupola (ill. 40). It is a perfect interplay of every part, yet each would be without any meaning by itself. How different it is from the centralised interior of the Renaissance, made up of separate entities, each of which could still have stood on its own. Borromini found no followers in Rome, though innumerable German eighteenth century interiors show his influence. Only once was Borromini connected with an important group of buildings, when he took over from Carlo Rainaldi at the church of S. Agnese in Piazza Navona. His chief contribution is the façade. Rainaldi's interior (ills. 13, 24), of 1645–50, is a square without aisles, because the piers supporting the dome have been slightly brought forward, it appears like an octagon. Rainaldi has hollowed out his piers even deeper than Bernini at St. Peter's, providing under the tall arcades space for altars with retables and, at the narrow ends, oratories. The heavy cornice advances and recedes in continuous movement.

At S. Agnese (ill. 21), as already at S. Ivo, Borromini's façade is unrelated to the interior. When it was begun by Borromini in 1652 Bernini's Fontana dei Fiumi with the obelisk was already there. Between them, these two great Roman masters have produced one of the city's finest piazzas (ills. 18, 21). The slight outward curve of the wings, offset by pilasters, responds to the concave façade, which seems to draw the whole piazza towards itself. Bernini's dream of a dome flanked by towers, unfulfilled at St. Peter's, has been realised by Borromini, with far-reaching consequences to the Baroque north of the Alps.

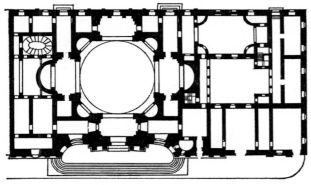

Rome, Sant'Agnese in Piazza Navona.

PIETRO BERETTINI DA CORTONA. The third

of the great revolutionaries of the Roman High Baroque—and also a non-Roman–is Pietro da Cortona (1596-1669). His name is derived from his native city. He built his first church, SS Martina e Luca, in Rome in 1635 (ill. 22). The curved front, the first of the Roman Baroque, is contemporary with Borromini's façade of the Oratorio dei Filippini. The coupled pilasters are like a solid frame. Immediately next to them, the wall curves inwards, to move forward again from a point marked on the ground floor by pillars and on the first storey by pilasters. The centre bay, round door and window, projects even further. Volutes give the tall narrow dome an almost bizarre appearance.

S. Maria Pace (ill. 35), Cortona has achieved a succession of curves, a backcloth from which the portico advances far into the piazza, linking inside and out.

NORTHERN ITALY. The dynamic variant of Italian Baroque culminates in the work of Guarino Guarini (1624–1685). From 1639 to 1647, Guarini, who had joined the Theatine order at an early age studied in Rome, chiefly theology, architecture and, above all, mathematics. His *Architettura civile*, published for the first time complete

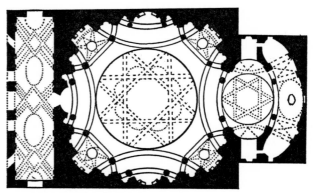

Turin, San Lorenzo.

in 1737, had already appeared as a volume of engravings nearly seventy years earlier (1688). Its influence, particularly on architects north of the Alps, was fundamental. In 1667, as engineer and architect to the Duke of Savoy, Guarini was put in charge of the Capella della SS. Sidone, at the east end of Turin Cathedral. The result was one of the most startling constructions of the entire Baroque, a dome formed of a network of thirty-six arches. A year later, 1668, Guarini began the church of S. Lorenzo, also in Turin (ills. 37, 39). The plan is octagonal, with concave sides opening out into convex compartments. To the north and south, these have been developed as flat recesses, in the diagonals as deep chapels, whose arcades are supported by detached columns–a highly original use of a Palladian motif, which also occurs in the treatment of the niches. The mood is one of restlessness and obscurity, from which the dome in no way detracts. Whether the ribs are completely detached or part of the masonry, the number of compartments in the ceiling, or even the height of the cupola, remains a complete mystery to the beholder. The play of light and shade and the intersection of regular and irregular forms seem governed by the laws of another world.

The second principal region-next to Turin and Piedmont-of the north Italian Baroque was Venice and the surrounding *terra firma*. S. Maria della Salute (ill. 43), is the work of Baldassare Longhena (1598–1682), a contemporary of Bernini. Six axial chapels project from the octagonal interior. Giant volutes support the drum. Next to Longhena's dynamic art the façade of another Venetian church, S. Moise (ill. 79), covered in decoration that adds no movement whatever, seems like a relic of a distant Mannerist past. At the same time, Lecce, in Apulia, produced one of the strangest flowers of European Baroque. The front of S. Croce (ill. 78) not merely combined seventeenth-century and Renaissance motifs, but even displays features of the despised art of the Middle Ages. With its tiny blind arcading below the gallery of consol figures supporting the balcony, the magnificent wheel window, and the gable, forms a unique ensemble of the styles of the past.

ITALIAN EIGHTEENTH-CENTURY CHUR-CHES. The leading Italian architect of the period was Filippo Juvara (1685–1735), a Sicilian, who spent ten years of his life in Rome. In 1714, Juvara moved to Turin, the capital of Savoy. Most European courts competed for his favour. He visited Portugal, England and France, and died in Madrid, busy with plans for a palace for Philip V. His most important church is the Superga, near Turin (ill. 170, below), undoubtedly the most outstanding Italian mountain church of the time. The enormous porch, the tall rotunda and the wings behind the towers, which mask the beginning of the convent, are linked by a wide, completely unbroken cornice. It is as if the Superga unites everything previous generations of architects strove for in their centralised buildings, from St. Peter's, S. Agnese or Palladio's Villa Rotonda to their Classic archetypes, such as the Pantheon.

The pilgrimage church of the Madonna di S. Luca (ill. 170, above), near Bologna, has none of the mature and sophisticated elegance of the Superga. Its broad front is flanked by the arms of a staircase whose Classic detail recalls Palladio.

In Rome, where it began, the Baroque produces another late flowering after the interval following the epoch of Bernini and Borromini. Once more, artists are spurred on by Papal patronage. But while Roman Rococo achieves some of its most outstanding triumphs in the Piazza San Ignazio and the Spanish Steps (ill. 115), it is already clear that the future belongs to the Classic taste, ardently championed by the Roman Academy. How far these two trends had diverged by the middle of the century can be seen in S. Giovanni in Laterano and S. Croce in Gerusalemne (ills. 130, 131). Both churches have a gallery of Saints above the roof-line, in the manner first evolved by Bernini at St. Peter's. But S. Croce is curved up to the very gable, while the front of the Lateran church, reminiscent of a triumphal arch, is flat. S. Croce (1743), belongs to the rearguard of the Baroque, S. Giovanni in Laterano (1735) is already a forerunner of the coming epoch.

BAROQUE CHURCHES IN FRANCE, ENGLAND AND SPAIN. When Salomon de Brosse built the new façade for the Paris church of S. Gervais (ill. 17), he was already conversant with the latest developments in Rome. His design still recalls Lescot's Louvre façade of 1546 rather than any Italian church. But we cannot ignore the Baroque language of the coupled pillars or the projecting cornice. At the church of Val-de-Grâce (ill. 80) in Paris, begun by Mansart (1645), the portico and the two flanking columns form almost a separate part. The façade, broken up by giant orders and recesses, has become a relief. Above the restrained gables, Lemercier has created an eminently Baroque dome with a widely projecting sculpture-supporting cornice, wedged between two rows of volutes, the uppermost of which carries another cornice with a whole crown of finials. The interior (ill. 31) follows Il Gesù, even in the uninterrupted line of the cornice near the dome. Between the piers–which, as at St. Peter's, have niches-stands a baldacchino, modelled on Bernini's. S. Sulpice (ill. 61), too, is Italian in the articulation of the walls, though Le Vau has based the plan on a Latin cross with aisles and ambulatory. The windows in the choir and the absence of barrel vaulting give the church an almost Gothic look.

The Dome des Invalides (1675-1706) can be described as the French version of St. Peter's. Its architect, Jules Hardouin-Mansart, went back to the centralised plans of the Renaissance. Yet he gave them an entirely new interpretation (ill. 63). Entrances to the pier chapels are now often placed diagonally, and are made so narrow that the most startling effects result. All the restlessness engendered by the soft curves of these chapels and their diagonal symmetry is offset by the most sober decorative detail imaginable. In the Dome des Invalides, Hardouin-Mansart has

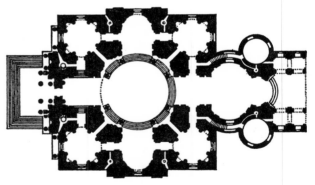

Paris, Dôme des Invalides.

created a temple of French absolutism rather than a Christian church. The magnificent façade, stepped back four times and clothed in a forest of pillars, is like that of a palace (ill. 62). Its controlled dynamism becomes more exuberant in the region of drum and dome where, particularly in the lantern, the effect is almost reminiscent of Borromini.

There could hardly be a greater contrast to the Invalides than Errard de Cheret's Eglise des Filles de l'Assomption (ill. 59), built between 1670 and 1676. Drum and dome, severe and plain except for the giant volutes at the lantern, almost dwarf the portico—a highly individual interpretation of Roman examples.

When Soufflot built Ste. Geneviève (ill. 235)—turned into the Pantheon by the Revolution—about a century later, he kept closely to Classic proportions. Only comparison with the Pantheon makes us realise how much Baroque movement there is in the façade of the Invalides. Soufflot's portico is no longer staggered, there is no articulation of the façade by coupled pillars. The columns are spaced at regular intervals, the walls are almost bare. French Baroque church architecture had never taken to the visionary abandon, the joyous piety, of its German or Italian equivalent. Towards the end, on the threshold of the French Revolution, it develops distinctly secular traits.

In England, St. Paul's Cathedral (1675–1710), begun by Sir Christopher Wren after the Great Fire, remained the only Baroque church of any size. While many cathedrals and abbeys were destroyed and replaced elsewhere during the Baroque, the English were faithful to the churches of their Catholic past. St. Paul's, too, does not break with tradition as much as the façade might suggest (ill. 29). The plan is cruciform, the aisles are continued beyond the crossing round the choir where, behind the altar, they form an apse in the space occupied in the medieval church by the Lady Chapel. This system of an elongated choir and wide transept, practically discarded by Italian Baroque architects, is entirely in keeping with the English tradition. The huge dome makes the crossing appear a central church of its own. In the façade Wren has succeeded in the synthesis of a dome and two towers, vainly attempted by

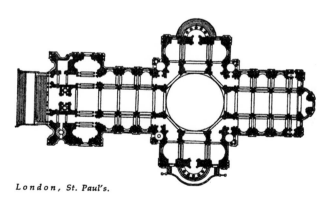

London, St. Paul's.

Bernini and only achieved on the comparatively small S. Agnese by Borromini. The proportions are not quite true in our illustration. In reality, the towers reach little more than half-way up the cupola. French influence is clear in the two-storied portico with the coupled pillars reminiscent of Perrault's Louvre façade. As at St. Peter's, the arrangement of the columns at portico and drum

differs, though Wren, unlike Maderna, has placed his single columns round the drum. His work thus has none of the almost titanic mood achieved by Michelangelo's use of a giant order. Yet there is strong vertical movement. The towers, surmounted by *tempietti* with broken entablatures and diagonally placed columns, are as fantastic as anything by Borromini.

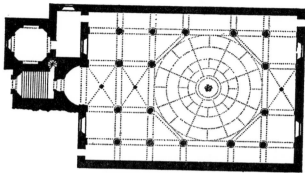

London, St. Stephen's, Walbrook.

Again, the treatment of the tower façades and the widely projecting transept arms is entirely unlike the work of Italian architects, who usually aim at compactness where the sides are concerned. In his city churches, Wren also interprets Continental inspirations very freely. His tower for St. Bride's, Fleet Street (ill. 68, right), is entirely Gothic in spirit, although the forms are Classic and the four superimposed *tempietti* would be unthinkable without Borromini. At St. Stephen's Walbrook (ill. 69), built 1672–87, Wren combined a centralised interior with aisles. Yet the particular construction of the dome—it is supported on pendentives which rest on free-standing columns—does away with the usual divisions. It is a variation of a theme first attempted by Guarini at S. Lorenzo, in Turin. During the late phase of the German Baroque it was to give rise to an infinity of interpretations. Yet the language of Wren's art was always restrained, and his decoration severely Classic.

English architects of all following generations found themselves caught up in the struggle between Baroque tendencies, the example of Palladio and Antiquity, and the Gothic tradition. At Christ Church, Spitalfields (ill. 226), Nicholas Hawksmoor combines a Gothic pointed spire with a Palladian entrance front. Unlike Wren and Hawksmoor, who had never been there, Thomas Archer (1668–1743) knew Italy well. Everthing he built is evidence that he was thoroughly conversant with the work of the great Roman and North Italian masters. At St. John's, Smith Square (1720), an *aedicula* has been placed in the centre of the gable, continuing the line of the columns of the portico (ill. 227). With its convex curves and the four cylindrical towers complete with pineapple finials and broken parapet, St. John's, Smith Square, is the most lavish example of the Baroque amongst London's parish churches. But, however rich it may be in memories of Borromini, the finials at once bring to mind Northern Gothic, nor is the debt to Antiquity any less obvious in the Classic detail.

Several chief influences are active in Spanish Boroque architecture. The first is Hereira's vast monastery palace, the Escorial. Versailles similarly demanded imitation, as did the careful articulation of French church façades. Italy's great contribution is the whole philosophy of Baroque architecture itself, in its two opposite poles, the Classic-monumental and the dynamic. In Spain, the dynamic, Borrominian element is further strengthened by an ancient and indigenous tradition of ornament, which had only gained in vigour by the Moorish accupation. In no other country does the Baroque display such a diversity of expression.

Spanish traits are more marked in churches than in palaces, whose character tends to be international. The Sagrario at Loyola, where the birthplace of the founder of the Jesuit order has been incorporated in a vast convent, was designed by Carlo Fontana in 1681. By the time it was finished, it had acquired more and more Spanish traits, not least in the dome (ill. 128), whose decoration, under Italian influence, is still comparatively restrained. At Santa Maria la Blanca (ill. 82, built 1659) in Seville we find for the first time as it were in its natural state—the shell form, which was later to appear in so many brilliant abstractions. In the sacristy of the Cartuja, Granada (ill. 83), the ornament has become less overpowering. It is concentrated on the piers, endowing them with an organic luxuriance, and the vaulting, where it appears as phantastic hieroglyphics. Cornices, without any direction, flow wavelike along the walls.

Like a huge retable, the reverse of Narciso Tomé's great screen, the 'Trasparente' in Toledo Cathedral, is divided into separate wings and stories, filled with sculpture. There is a glazed opening below the group of the Last Supper, exactly in the place where the Sacrament appears on the High Altar. Worshippers in the ambulatory could thus take part in the Mass no less than the congregation in the main body of the church. An opening, invisible from below, has been made in the cross-vaulting of the ambulatory opposite this 'two-sided alter' (see drawing) and a golden light flows through it on the statues and in the Blessed Sacrament. The age saw nothing wrong in the use of such theatrical devices. On the contrary the worshipper longed for a mood of wonder in the church. Amongst South German Baroque masters, the Asam brothers employed similar effects.

But the profusion of ornament or sculpture is mostly confined to the interior of Spanish churches. The lavish façades of Spanish Late Gothic, with an overlay of Boroque articulation, live on in Latin America (ills. 86, 87). In Spain itself, the façade of the church, though far from plain, owes its character to dynamic curves rather than decoration. The west front of Valencia Cathedral (ill. 125), hemmed in between Miguelete tower and chapter house, seems to struggle against its very setting. The flanks press forward and yet have to draw in again. The centre bay, left behind, curves outward. Even where a more horizontal expansion is possible, as at Murcia Cathedral (ill. 80) the impression of conflicting movement remains.

On the façade of Santiago de Compostela (ill. 84), which Casas y Nuova placed before the Romanesque Portico della Gloria in 1738, Baroque love of elaborate contortion yields to a powerful vertical dynamism. The entire front, deeply hollowed out and opening even further into doors, windows and recesses under the round-headed arches, still has all the transcendentalism of a Gothic cathedral.

Spanish influence was not confined to South America, of whose treasury of Baroque building only a few examples can be shown in these pages (ills. 85–87). Sicily and Southern Italy, for many years under Spanish rule, developed a highly original Spanish-Italian style (ill. 81). At Cadiz Cathedral, Vicente Acero has created one the most outstanding interiors of the time (ill. 139). The aisles are taken across the wide transept and, at the choir, become ambulatory with radiating chapels. The transept itself merges with the octagonal Capilla Mayor. All the movement of this succession of interpenetrating compartments is expressed in the shape of the diagonal piers that seem buffeted into their positions by the constant flow of a mighty stream.

In Portugal, the synthesis of landscape and architecture has produced an axial lay-out of startling elegance in the pilgrimage church of Bom Jesus do Monte, near Braga (ill. 178). Cascade-like a two-armed stair-case leads down from the church. No description could do justice to the ever-changing vistas, produced by the succession of diagonal and axial viewpoints.

PALACE AND DOMESTIC ARCHITECTURE IN FRANCE, ENGLAND, ITALY AND SPAIN.

Baroque domestic architecture was at first based on North

Toledo, the "Trasparente" in the ambulatory. On the right the opening in the pier towards the High Altar, on the left the pierced vaulting compartment with the Baroque dormer, invisible from below.

Italian examples. Though the church architecture of the new epoch had its origins in Rome, Roman streets were still at a fortress-like severity. Yet in Northern Italy, Palladio and Sansovino had already opened out their façades into arches and loggias during the Late Renaissance. The Palladian motif of an arch supported by columns brought about a revolution. The pillar even replaced the heavy pier in the arcaded courtyard (ills. 16, 88). Roman severity had its counterpart north of the Alps in ascetic simplicity of the convent at Seckau, in Styria, or Skokloster, in Sweden (ills. 7, above and below). It is not least some indication of the enormous influence of the Escorial. Though built after Maderna's and Bernini's churches, one arcaded front of the Palazzo Barberini (ill. 15) with its half columns and projecting portico must have caused a sensation in contemporary Rome. In his later palaces, Bernini returns to Roman earnestness. The trends that found expression in the Palazzo Barberini develop to the full in the Northern provinces. Baldassare Longhena's Palazzo Pesaro (ill. 42), is typical of the Venetian High Baroque.

But it needed a different political climate to produce the Royal palace *par excellence*. The second decisive change happened in France. Here, as throughout Europe, the reaction against Mannerism had set in. One could hardly imagine anything more severe than the façade of the Palais de la Monnaie (ill. 58) in Avignon. The swags accentuate rather than invade the impenetrability of the background. Yet North Italian influence proved irresistible,

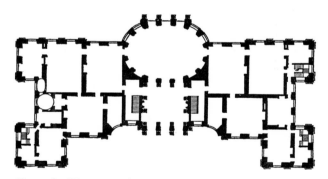

Vaux-le-Vicomte. The earliest example of an "enfilade", an axially planned interior.

not least because it met the demands of an aristocracy which had come to look for more splendour and ostentation. The Italian villa had normally been of modest dimensions. In its French version, it appears complete with pavilions and *cour d'honneur.* Now we find the 'Enfilade'–a suite of intercommunicating rooms, affording long vistas– and the axial orientation of palace and park. Such a system could only develop in the country of the absolute monarchy, where everything centred on the Crown. Cheverny, near Blois, completed 1634, is a typical example (ill. 53, above). The severe façade, flanked by two pavilions and

except for the central tower without any projections, contrasts with an almost bizarre roof-line. At Dampierre-sur-Boutonne (ill. 52), the pavilion system has been carried further. Corner blocks project, pilasters rise along the centre bays. Movement has been transferred from the region of the roof to the façade. The pavilions, at Cheverny distinguished chiefly by their roofs, have become separate buildings and form the *cour d'honneur.* A central axis leading from the main block, the *corps de logis* to the gates in one direction and to the park on the other, links the building with the landscape. The distinction between indoors and out gradually fades.

When François Mansart enlarged Blois (ill. 45) in 1635, he too arranged his new buildings as a *cour d'honneur.* As in the town palaces of the time, called hotels (ill. 45), there is a strong central emphasis, entirely in the spirit of the Baroque.

The new east front of the Louvre (ill. 67, above) is an early indication of the changes in French taste round the middle of the century. The delight in Baroque curves (one of the most charming examples is Vaux-le-Vicomte, 1652) has gone. The curve is now considered ugly, the articulation of the roof rejected. Perrault's winning Louvre design, executed 1667–70, had had to compete against Bernini's. The two upper stories have been dissolved into a colonnade of coupled Corinthian pillars. But though Italian dynamism has gone, the façade is Baroque in its depth, in its interpretation as a series of superimposed relief. The façade of the Hôtel des Invalides (ill. 67, below), built by Liberal Bruant 1671–1674, is almost completely bare. Like Perrault, Bruant disdains pavilions, agitated rooflines or curves. He is already a forerunner of the Classic revival, which was to assert itself in France long before elsewhere. Nearly every Baroque palace in France, and indeed throughout Europe, has been touched by the spirit of Versailles. The scheme of a house set on an axial approach with a park beyond, first evolved in the Italian villa, has been developed in France into an elaborate network full of political symbolism (ills. 48/49). Two straight roads radiate from the centre of Versailles, the bedchamber of the king in the *corps de logis.* The park, also, is orientated towards this focal point. The vast *cour d'honneur* in front of the *corps de logis* is staggered first from the Place d'Armes, where the three roads divide, to the Cour Royale, and again towards the Cour de Marbre (ill. 44) with Le Vau's façades. Behind are the state rooms of the palace, the king's bedroom and the Galerie des Glaces (ill. 50).

The garden front was given its present form in 1679 by Jules Hardouin-Mansart, who added the two wings, thus extending the façade to a length of nearly 1,900 ft. As at Perrault's Louvre, there are no curves. Movement is achieved solely through the columnation. Large openings relieve any effect of heaviness in the rusticated base. Sculpture on parapet and balconies achieves an elegant harmony between verticals and horizontals.

In the chapel (ill. 51) at Versailles, Classic and dynamic elements combine in a rather unusual manner. The arcades and columns of the nave, which is continued into an ambulatory, are of an almost Roman dignity. Yet the vaulting is of a strangely Gothic restlessness. No less Gothic in spirit are the tail roof and the flying buttresses.–Delamaire's façade of the Hôtel Soubise (ill. 229) in Paris, and even more, the palace at Compiègne (ill. 110), belong to a new and more severe epoch. The windows have become square and sober, sculpture has almost disappeared.

Nancy is amongst the last of the great manifestations of Baroque absolutism. The large octagonal Place Stanislas is linked by the long and narrow Place Carrière with the Palais du Gouvernement (ill. 214). The whole lay-out, with the transition from enclosed to open spaces and, finally, from the planned townscape to an equally planned landscape is almost unsurpassed, even in the eighteenth century (ill. 215).

In England, the first architect of the new era was Inigo Jones. From 1613–14, the 'Surveyor of the King's Works' had visited Italy. The Queen's House, Greenwich (ill. 70, above) is the first example of a building of Classic compactness with an open Palladian loggia. The whole lay-out must have appeared revolutionary at the time. In 1619, when Roman street fronts were still severe and restrained, Inigo Jones created the first Baroque façade–London's Banqueting Hall for the never-completed Palace of Whitehall (ill. 14, below). Though two different orders, Ionic below and Corinthian above, suggest two floors, the building only has one storey. At the centre bays, the pilasters swell into half columns.

Few, if any, other buildings can be attributed to Inigo Jones with any degree of certainty. Raynham Hall (ill. 102, above), in Norfolk, undoubtedly shows his influence. Again, there is strong articulation–half-columns, stone quoins–though hardly any movement. The Classic gables form a strange contrast with the rather Dutch volutes. The Dutch House (ill. 55) at Kew, built 1631, nearly twenty years later than the Queen's House at Greenwich, still preserves the form of the English country house before Inigo Jones, Palladianism, and the Baroque.

It was left to Sir Christopher Wren, already of the third generation of the Baroque, to build on a scale comparable to the vast schemes of the Continent. Wren virtually rebuilt Hampton Court and added domes, chapel, hall and colonnades to Inigo Jones' Greenwich Hospital, now the Royal Naval College (ills. 70 above, and 71) on the banks of the Thames. Again, there are twin pillars, reminiscent of French examples on the portico and dome at St. Paul's. With its rich shadow effects, the façade appears like a succession of superimposed reliefs, from the colonnade of the ground floor and the gabled and hollowed-out wall above, to the broken entablature of the drum. Severe Doric detail is also used on another of Wren's buildings, the Chelsea Hospital (ill. 86), where a giant order extends from base to cornice. Before, his rather restrained manner, in which, like Bruant at the Hôtel des Invalides, he is concerned with clarity of disposition rather than ornament; Wren had opened out his façades into arcaded loggias (Trinity College Cambridge, ill. 70 below, and Abingdon Town Hall, ill. 65, built by Christopher Kempster in the same year, 1676, obviously under Wren's influence).

The eighteenth century inaugurated one of the great events in English architecture, Blenheim Palace, begun by Vanbrugh (1664–1726) in 1705, as a present from Queen Anne to the first Duke of Marlborough, victor of the battle of Blenheim (1704). Vanbrugh, who, like many English architects, was a brilliant amateur, had only begun his building career shortly before with his design for Castle Howard. His three great palaces–the third is Seaton Delaval (ill. 106) in Northumberland–with their vast courtyards are like English interpretations of Versailles. Turrets, an integral part of the English manor house of the Middle Ages and the Renaissance, had been dispensed with by Italian Ba-

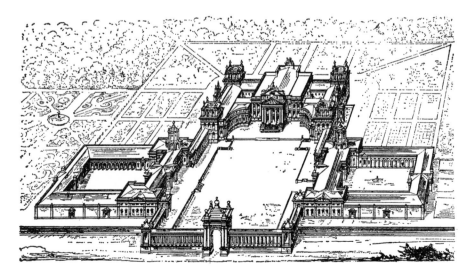

Blenheim Palace, Baroque in its lay-out rather than in the Classic detail.

roque architects and their Central European followers. Vanbrugh, varying a French theme, retains them by taking his corner pavilions far above the main roofline: in secular architecture, as in the church, the medieval tradition lives on in England.

The Palladian reaction against Vanbrugh's powerful Baroque gesture soon followed. Chiswick House (ill. 101), begun by Lord Burlington in 1725, is modelled on Palladio's Villa Rotunda at Vicenza. Yet the diagonal runs of the outdoor staircase are entirely Baroque and in sharp contrast to Palladio's axial approach. In England, where balance rather than exuberance is the key to architecture, four brilliant Scotsmen, the Adam brothers, became the chief exponents of the new epoch. Eventually, their influence was hardly less marked on the Continent. The giant orders and the detail round the windows at Harewood House (ill. 186 below), built by Robert Adam c. 1760, appear almost delicately drawn. Yet despite this contrast to Vanbrugh's massed effects, the wings, rising above the cornice, have again come to resemble turrets.

The Senate House (ill. 229 below) at Cambridge, with its gay and elegant façade, might almost be a North Italian villa. It is the work of James Gibbs (1674–1754), who, like few of his fellow architects in Britain, knew Rome well. In his Radcliffe Camera (ill. 231), at Oxford, the Baroque trend asserts itself once more in eighteenth century England. Some of the detail is reminiscent of Wren's work at Greenwich, though the coupled pillars, instead of lending vertical emphasis, serve to create the impression of volume.

In town planning, the Classic influence was singularly happy in England. The Circus (ill. 230, below) at Bath is only one of many examples. Though the curved front appears throughout Europe, it has nowhere been adopted to the same degree, or quite as successfully. In the façade of the Dublin Custom House (ill. 230, above), Baroque elements linger on, though the final triumph of the Classic Revival is obiously close at hand. Gone is the articulation of the walls, the corner blocks no longer assert themselves; yet the columns round the tall drum of the dome have retained their Baroque rhythm.

In Italy, the eighteenth century took up the challenge of Versailles. The North, far more inclined to display and ostentation than Rome, leads once more. Filippo Juvara's staircase in the Palazzo Madama (ill. 89) in Turin was to become epoch-making. The simple hunting boxes of the Piedmontese and Venetian nobility are turned into minor palaces, such as the Palazzo Stupinigi (ill. 193), near Turin, transformed by Juvara in 1729, complete with an elaborate system of *cour d'honneur*. The scale recalls Versailles, the dramatic treatment Borromini. At the centre is a magnificent oval saloon (ill. 193).

The illusionist paintings at the Villa Lecchi (ill. 197), near Brescia, just as startling, suggest a princely palace rather than a summer residence. At the Villa Pisani (ill. 185, above) at Strà, near Venice, built in 1735 for the Doge, we find the same trend as in contemporary Roman archi-

tecture; Juvara's dynamism is gradually yielding to Palladian forms. In Ferdinando Fuga's Palazzo della Consulta (ill. 108), plastic accents are restricted to the doors; elsewhere the decoration might be no more than delicately engraved. Hardly any traces of movement are left on the façade of the royal palace at Caserta, near Naples (1752). Yet the park (ill. 183) is magnificently exuberant, the interior is a triumph of the Baroque art of space (ills. 194, 195). The octagon at the top of the monumental staircase affords ever-changing vistas along the obliquely placed piers.

In Spain the Audiencia (ill. 14, above), in Granada, built 1584, is an early attempt to overcome the severity of official court architecture, whose pattern was set by the Escorial. The taste of the nobility was less austere. The palace of the Marques des Dos Aguas (ill. 201), in Valencia, belongs to the end of the Spanish Baroque. Though the walls are still flat, they have been covered by a veritable riot of ornament, which does not even stop at the Tabernacle with the statue of the Virgin.

The great royal palaces are more restrained. La Granja (ill. 104, below), nearly 4,000 feet up in the Sierra da Guadarrama, was to provide the king with monastic seclusion. Yet it grew into a Spanish Versailles, complete with *cour d'honneur* and axially planned park. But while the chapel of the Roi Soleil occupied a very subordinate place in the general scheme, the domed church at La Granja stands at the centre of the *cour d'honneur*. The garden front, with its lively rhythm of pilasters, coupled pilasters and half-columns, was completed in 1736 by Sacchetti to Juvara's designs.

The royal palace in Madrid, also the work of Juvara and Sacchetti, eventually took the form of a square block, built round an enclosed courtyard (ill. 111, below). Without projecting wings or a *court d'honneur*, it resembles Versailles less than any other royal residence. By endowing it with such fortress-like severity, accentuated by the enormous rusticated base and the complete absence of sculpture on the principal storey, Sacchetti has followed the trend away from the Baroque to the final triumph of Classic form. It is a development that begins already before the middle of the eighteenth century.

The summer palace of the kings of Portugal at Queluz (ill. 174) near Lisbon is, like La Granja, a mixture of French and Spanish forms. The grouping of the low blocks, surmounted by a variety of gables, is singularly charming.

THE SEVENTEENTH AND EIGHTEENTH CENTURIES IN GERMANY. The façade of Elias Holl's Zeughaus (ill. 8), built 1602, has an almost explosive force. Broken pediments continue up to the very top, each storey asserts itself anew. Volutes seem to hold the building together like a vice. At a time when S. Susanna (ill. 9) astonished Rome, Holl's genius created a specifically German language of form, symbolic perhaps of an age torn by religious strife.

The Rathaus, built 1610–20, shows quite a different aspect of the master's work (ill. 6). It rises compact and block-like, its façade articulated by graphic means rather than sculpture. The slightly restless mood suggested by the taller windows and the mere simulation of a centre block is like an anticipation of the new age.–Plain walls that announce the final break with Mannerism.

At Seckau (ill. 7, above), austerity is carried even further. Severe and unadorned, the façade recalls the Escorial. It is such walls, blank like a new canvas, that signify the beginning of the Baroque, not the pre-Baroque exuberance of the Augsburg Zeughaus (ill. 8).

While the Baroque could flourish in Italy and Spain, France and England, the Thirty Years' War, and the poverty and lethargy it brought, left Elias Holl without any immediate successors. It is therefore not surprising that the first Baroque church on German soil, Salzburg Cathedral (ill. 12), started 1614, was also the only one for over half a century, until 1668, the year work was begun at Passau.

The next steps follow after the interval of the Thirty Years' War. The old generation of German architects is no longer active, the new has not yet come. The architects of Passau, St. Florian and the Munich Theatinerkirche (ills. 90–92) are therefore again Italians.

The new century saw a Germany at last freed from the spell of the Thirty Years' War. The first generation of German Baroque architects was ready, and royal patrons could now look to German artists to carry out their ambitious schemes. It is characteristic of the age that so many designs for churches, convents, palaces and whole cities never materialised because they were too vast, utterly unrealistic in their very concept. Others remained unfinished. Yet many of them did fortunately materialise, and survive to bear witness to the genius of an epoch unparalleled in Germany since the great medieval cathedrals.

JOHANN BERNHARD FISCHER VON ERLACH.

Shortly before the beginning of the eighteenth century, Johann Bernhard Fischer von Erlach inaugurates the new era in art with two Salzburg churches, which both combine turrets with a curved façade at the smaller Dreifaltigkeitskirche, the curve recedes, at the Collegiate Church (ill. 120), the façade projects with powerful plasticity, relieved by arched windows and checked by the broad cornice. Parapets crown the turrets, saints stand above the diagonal volutes. Something entirely different from the flat façades of the Italian Baroque architects active in Germany had been achieved. Fischer (1656–1723), whose three years' stay in Rome had given him a thorough knowledge of the Baroque, combines in his work memories of Bernini and Borromini, Maderna and Cortona. Yet if we look for an earlier equivalent to the forceful modelling of the projecting centre block of the Collegiate Church, we are–as in the case of Weingarten and Wibling (ills. 121, 133)–more likely to find it in the apses of the German Romanesque than in Italy. When Fischer designed Klessheim (ill. 100) soon afterwards, he proved himself equally *au fait* with contemporary

French art: the combination of four columns with round-headed arches above a rusticated base recalls Versailles. His elaborate relief-like treatment of the garden front was also unusually advanced for early eighteenth century Germany. Everything is orientated towards the centre, though buildings and landscape form one composition, linked by the curve of the parapet. Fischer, official architect to the Imperial Court, was the first German artist to be ennobled.

Fischer's two great projects for the Austrian Court, the Hofburg and Schönbrunn, planned on a scale vastly surpassing Versailles, did not materialise according to his intentions. Both belong to those fantastic Baroque schemes which, perhaps, were never really thought possible by their architects. Schönbrunn, built to Fischer's second design (ill. 177) was already altered by his son Josef Emanuel, then by Pacassi and again c. 1820. But the lay-out with the vast *court d'honneur* and the handsome *corps de logis* are unquestionably Fischer's. The master's design for the Hofburg has disappeared. Only the long, low stable block–its length of nearly 400 yds. gives some idea of the vast dimensions of the whole scheme–was built by himself. Work on the library wing, Hofbibliothek (ill. 136) did not begin until 1723, shortly after Fischer's death, under his son Josef Emanuel. The façade echoes memories of Bernini's first designs for the Louvre, which had made such a lasting impression on Fischer. The interior is something entirely new: a temple of learning, serene as a church.

LUCAS VON HILDEBRANDT.

The Peterskirche in Vienna by Lucas von Hildebrandt (1666–1745), is contemporary with Fischer's Salzburg churches. Hildebrandt, a native of Genoa and of part-Italian origin, had been a military engineer before he settled in Vienna in 1696. Five years later he was appointed official court architect. He was trained in Rome and also had a thorough knowledge of the state of architecture in Northern Italy. The oval interior of the Peterskirche recalls motifs used by Guarini, the façade (ill. 95) is reminiscent of Borromini's S. Agnese (ill. 21), though far more dynamic in the evasion of right angles. Hildebrandt is more agile and light-hearted than Fischer, whose concepts are always on an 'Imperial' scale. The staircase at Schloss Mirabell (ill. 99) and the Belvedere (ill. 174, above) on the one hand, the Karlskirche and the Hofbibliothek on the other, represent two poles of German eighteenth century Baroque. It is no accident that these contrasts should reveal themselves with such clarity first in Vienna, where the whole social and political background was so exceptionally favourable to the arts.

Patronised by the aristocracy, foremost by Prince Eugen, Hildebrandt created palaces which were to become almost archetypal for the coming Rococo. His additions to Schloss Mirabell (ill. 99) include a staircase of straight runs, arranged round a well. Simple enough compared to the Belvedere, the Palais Daun-Kinsky, Göttweig or Pommersfelden–yet the flowing parapet with Raphael Donner's *putti* makes it one of the most delightful solutions of its kind.

Hildebrandt's most important work, Prince Eugen's garden palace, is unrivalled in Viennese palace architecture. The commission was for a modest dwelling, which Hildebrandt placed at the foot of the hill, and another building with state apartments, not intended to be lived in permanently. The two 'Belvederes' separated by parterres with fountains and basins, are axially orientated. There is no *cour d'honneur* (ill. 174, above), avenues of trees take the place of flanking walls. A huge basin, almost a lake, mirrors the façade. This typically Baroque device has been used innumerable times by later architects. The opening out of the centre pavilion marks another decisive step in the development of the German Baroque mansion. The rooms merge, and seem to continue into the vista of courtyard and park. While the staircases reflect the influence of Turin and Genoa, the façade suggests French examples, such as Cheverny (ill. 53) with no less than seven pavilions, each with its own roof, a typical French Baroque château before the triumph of the simple Classic outline. But Hildebrandt, with polygonal towers and a succession of roofs and gables above the porch, has achieved a far livelier solution. The Belvedere is no more 'modelled' on Cheverny than the Peterskirche on S. Agnese. At the most, we can say that an age-old motif has been varied with super mastery. With Fischer and Hildebrandt, German Baroque has made its spectacular entrée into European art.

THE DIENTZENHOFER FAMILY. A second important centre in the first phase of German Baroque was Prague, where, as early as 1621, Andrea Spezza had designed the loggia of the Palais Waldstein. The resemblance to the courtyards of Milan and Genoa is obvious (ill. 16 above, 88). Italian influence, here as in Vienna, was very strong throughout the seventeenth century. Its culmination was perhaps Guarini's project for a church. The plan, two intersecting ovals, was revolutionary for Prague. Though never executed, it had a profound effect on the work of the Dientzenhofers, a Bavarian family of architects settled in Prague. With St. Nikolaus-auf-der-Kleinseite (ill. 93), begun in 1703, Christoph Dientzenhofer (1665–1722) achieved for the first time a dynamic interior. The plan of the nave still follows Il Gesù. But a new impetus has taken hold of the conventional pattern. The piers are without exception placed diagonally, linked by bulging galleries. The figures of saints below seem to take up the all-uniting movement that pulsates along the walls. Only the ceiling defies the architect's ingenuity; it remains a simple barrel vault. A few years later, in the church at Brevnov, near Prague, Dientzenhofer, following Guarini, continues the interpenetration of the four ovals of the nave into the roof.

Christoph's brother Johann (d. 1728) uses this form in the convent at Banz. Balthasar Neumann's magnificent spatial compositions are to no small degree indebted to Banz and the work of the Dientzenhofers in general. In 1711, Johann Dientzenhofer began Schloss Weissenstein near Pommersfelden, the summer residence of the Bishop of Bamberg and

Elector of Mainz, Lother Franz von Schönborn. This highly gifted amateur and patron of the arts, who, in his own words was "possessed by building fever", took a hand in the design of the unique staircase (ill. 190) which surpasses anything built in Vienna. The last outstanding architect amongst the Dientzenhofers was Christoph's son Kilian Ignaz (1689/90–1751) who, in 1727, added choir dome and tower to St. Nicholas-auf-der-Kleinseite, the church begun by his father twenty-four years earlier (ill. 114). The façade of St. Nicholas Alstadt (1732–37), a church built on a central plan, is brilliantly accentuated by sculpture and coupled pillars. The portico is in the tradition of Fischer von Erlach (ill. 94).

ANDREAS SCHLÜTER. Schlüter's origins and early life are obscure. But we do know that the master was a sculptor, was born in Danzig c. 1660, and was called to the Berlin Court 1694. Two years later he travelled in Italy, from 1698 he was working at the Zeughaus and the Royal Palace in Berlin (ill. 96, 97). His treatment of the façade is Roman rather than French. Fischer went to Berlin to see Schlüter's work. In the vast, superhuman dimensions of their buildings, both artists are in the direct succession of Bernini and Michelangelo. Schlüter's work in Berlin came to an end in 1706. In 1714, he went to Russia at the request of Peter the Great. A year later he died. Practically all his work was destroyed during the last war, or has fallen into ruins since.

DANIEL PÖPPELMANN. Daniel Pöppelmann, architect to Augustus the Strong of Saxony, was born in Herford, Westphalia, in 1662. Though, like Schlüter, Fischer and Hildebrandt, of the first generation of Baroque architects, his mature phase lasted somewhat longer. When he took up his appointment in 1704, the three other great masters of the Baroque had already developed their own style.
Within the orbit of Vienna and Berlin and working for a monarch fascinated by Versailles, Pöppelmann brought an entirely different approach to each task, without at the same time giving up his highly personal manner. One of his most famous creations is the 'Zwinger' (ill. 188) on the banks of the Elbe. For the first time, what has hitherto only been attempted in wood, as an ephemeral decoration for some fête champêtre, has been given more permanent form in brick and stone. The 'Zwinger' consists of a series of pavilions, linked by single-storied arcaded halls. It is a brilliant variation of the medieval jousting yard. However much Pöppelmann has learned from Vienna and Paris—the unrestrained ecstacy, the tingling vibration of every form, are no-one's but his own—Schloss Pommersfelden shows the artist in a different, though no less sensitive, mood (ill. 105). A variety of motifs—several Corinthian orders, pagoda roofs and inward curving cornices—has been combined to a delightful synthesis.

GERMAN EIGHTEENTH-CENTURY ABBEYS AND ABBEY CHURCHES. Jacob Prandtauer's abbeys, complete with church, library, state apartments and living quarters, represent an entirely new development in German monastic architecture. Their lay-out–St. Florian, near Linz on the plain (ill. 118), or Melk, rising dramatically above the Danube (ill. 119)–and dimensions, recall Versailles or the Escorial, their style Hildebrandt or Dientzenhofer. But any similarity with other buildings ends here. Prandtauer, a simple stonemason from the Tyrol, with little, if any, Classic learning, could absorb and transform these influences with an almost unequalled imagination. The grouping at Melk, the brilliant juxtaposition of building and landscape anticipates Juvara's Superga, near Turin, by fifteen years. In the interior of the church (ill. 122) Prandtauer still follows the Italian architects of Passau and Salzburg, though the dynamism is new. The curving galleries are an important step in the dissolution of the walls.

Ettal (ill. 118, below), built around the–originally Gothic-centralised church, was begun by Enrico Zuccali in 1710. The present dome and interior, the work of Joseph Schmuzer, date from 1745, when the earlier buildings were burned down. Since 1740, Schmuzer had been in charge at Weingarten. But the Benedictine abbey there was never completed. With its gardens and *cour d'honneur* it was a typical Baroque fantasy, never very likely to materialise (see drawing). Only the part to the left of the church was finished. The history of the church itself is rather obscure. Some of the architects involved–Kaspar Moosbrugger, Johann Jakob Herkomer, Franz Beer and Donate Frisoni–belong, with the exception of the last-named, to the so-called Vorarlberg School, whose influence extends throughout the region of Lake Constance over Germany, Austria and Switzerland. The Vorarlberg School remained faithful to the example of Il Gesù. Yet Weingarten is already far removed from its archetype. The piers (ill. 123) have advanced from the walls, no cornice unites them any longer. It is the first step towards the free-standing supports of Neumann's churches. The curving front between the towers (ill. 121) recalls Fischer's Collegiate Church in Salzburg, whose influence may also account for some of the Italian features in the interior.

St. Gallen and Einsiedeln are other attempts at linking the practical advantages of a basilica with the majesty of a centralised interior (ills. 152, 153). The pilgrimage church at Einsiedeln, like Vierzehnheiligen more than twenty years later, represents the problem of two focal points, one for the High Altar, and one for the Mercy Chapel. Moosbrugger places the chapel in an octagon at the western end of the church, and vaults the nave bays with two domes. The Asam brothers' plasterwork and the delightful wrought-iron gates complete this brilliant solution of an extremely difficult problem.

Ottobeuren with its Kaisersaal ('Emperor's Halls', a hall with sixteen wooden statues of Habsburg Emperors) and library is the most lavish of the South German Baroque monasteries. Johann Michael Fischer's church, begun 1737 (ill. 144), is, in its general mood of gay piety, not unlike the slightly smaller convent church at Zwiefalten (ill. 145) by the same master. Though similar to Weingarten in the triapsial arrangement of transept and choir, Ottobeuren makes no claim to monumentality. Light floods the nave, and the walls are deliberately obscured by the curving galleries that link the seemingly free-standing twin columns. As at Weingarten, there is no cornice. The example of Il Gesù counts no longer. Zwiefalten is structurally less complicated, though the exuberant rocaille decoration, which overflows to arcades, altar, font and organ, wiping out all distinction between painting and architecture (ill. 161) and the ironwork (ill. 154) are but the perfect complement to Fischer's work.

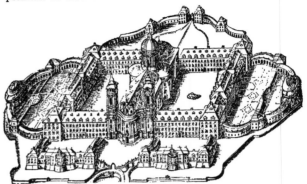

Weingarten. The original design.

THE ASAM BROTHERS. In common with many leading German Baroque artists, the Asam brothers were of humble artisan origin. Unlike the Viennese Baroque masters and Balthasar Neumann, they were never raised to the nobility. Yet, though they never built on a monumental scale, their effect has been far-reaching in the extreme. Cosmas Damian Asam (1696–1739) was chiefly architect and painter, his brother Egid Quirin (1697-1750) sculptor and stucco worker. Jointly, they decorated many churches (ills. 152, 159). Ills. 126 and 127 show two small churches which are entirely their own work. Both are amongst the jewels of the Baroque. In the Benedictine convent at Weltenburg on the Danube, a recessed oval–known to the brothers from their journey to Rome as the basic Italian plan of the time—leads into the unique altar space (ill. 126). Between the twisted columns, St. George, the patron Saint, emerges out of the light to kill the dragon, while a frightened princess looks on. The effect of a vision is complete. Toledo's 'Trasparente' (ill. 77) achieves the same intentions, not least because the source of light is also hidden. In the semi-darkness of the narrow nave of the tiny Johann-Nepomuk-Kirche, built by the brothers next to their own house (ill. 127) the superb artistry of the plasterwork breaks down all barriers between reality and illusion.

Yet, working for other architects, the manner of the Asam brothers is far more down-to-earth, of a comparatively ordinary gaiety rather than mystic ecstacy.

BALTHASAR NEUMANN. The leading artist of the second generation of the German Baroque is Balthasar

Neumann, one of the outstanding individualities of the whole epoch. He was born in 1687 in Eger, Bohemia, and, like Hildebrandt, he was for many years an engineer in the Austrian army. In 1719, when Johann Philip Franz von Schönborn, Prince Bishop of Würzburg, entrusted him with the design for a new palace, Neumann had reached the rank of captain. On campaigns throughout Europe he had acquired a thorough knowledge of architecture. This knowledge he increased considerably when his patron sent him to Paris in 1723 to discuss his plans with the leading masters of the time. He also visited Vienna and had a vast international correspondence. Through the ceaseless building activity of the Schönborn family, Neumann was gradually placed in charge over a vast network of civilian and military schemes. A scientific mind and a sense of beauty have rarely met to quite the same degree in a Baroque artist. He died in 1753 at the peak of his career.

His principal work–and one of the most outstanding creations of European Baroque–is the Würzburg Residenz (ills. 124, 189, 191, 192) which occupied him for several decades. The wings are grouped round a *cour d'honneur* and four inner courtyards with a pavilion at the centre of each side. The garden front is of a charm comparable to Hildebrandt, whose inspiration is also evident in the changing silhouette of the roof. Again like Hildebrandt, Neumann gives his staircase a central position. The two main stories of the garden pavilion are taken up by the Kaisersaal, the 'Emperor's Hall' (ill. 192). Where the dome is not pierced by windows, Tiepolo's illusionist fresco continues the work of the architect. The chapel (ill. 124) recalls Dientzenhofer at Banz. Interpenetrating oval bays cause a veritable whirlpool of movement, the arrangement of the columns in the ambulatory shows that the spirit of the originators of Baroque dynamism, Borromini and Guarini, has also been

centre of a large oval. A smaller oval follows towards the entrance, while the apse is developed as a second centre (ill. 141). Galleries form the only link between piers and wall. The windows were not given their disturbingly harsh outline until long after Neumann's death, when the church was at last completed. The church of the Benedictine abbey at Neresheim (ill. 151), which Neumann began shortly before he died is like a Classic interpretation of Vierzehnheiligen. There is a simple nave bisected by a transept. But to Neumann, the basilica favoured by the architects of the Vorarlberg School is merely the framework for a succession of ovals. Light flows in through the tall windows with an intensity that breaks down all barriers between indoors and out. Vierzehnheiligen, with its plasterwork by Johann Michael Feichtmayr and Johann Georg Üblher, is still very much of this world. Neresheim's beauty is of a more transcendental kind. It is as if a new lucidity had been brought to bear on Baroque restlessness.

DOMINIKUS ZIMMERMANN. Dominikus Zimmermann (1685–1766) began as a stonemason. With his painter brother Johann Baptist he created two of the most charming of the smaller pilgrimage churches of the whole epoch. At the same time he developed with Balthasar Neumann a new type of church with freestanding piers. In the Wieskirche at Steingaden and at Steinhausen (ill. 148) the walls have been reduced to little more than a thin shell. In the Wieskirche, begun 1745, a long aisled and galleried choir (ills. 147, 149) adjoins the main oval. But though Zimmermann achieves his incredible vistas, his uninterrupted flow of space, through an almost Gothic elimination of the wall, he is never reduced to mere calculation, like Guarini or some of the other great Italian architects. Throughout, Steingaden and the Wieskirche preserve a quality of organic growth.

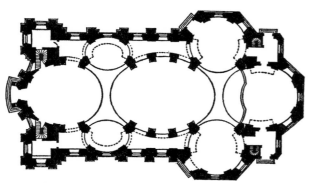

Vierzehnheiligen.

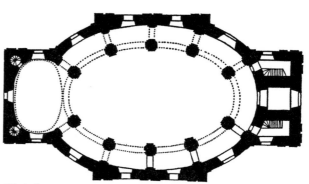

Steinhausen.

active. Their systems are interpreted by Neumann with a lightness and delicacy that allows the free flow of space. Vierzehnheiligen and Neresheim (ills. 140–142, 151) must be considered the most outstanding German contribution to the church architecture of the Baroque. Vierzehnheiligen is a pilgrimage church, built around the altar of the Fourteen Helpers in Need. Neumann has made the Altar the

Birnau, begun 1746 by Peter Thumb, is the end of an epoch. The great search of the Baroque for an Einheitsraum, the unified interior, has ended in a simple hall (ill. 157), whose applied decoration has little bearing on its architecture. Another late style comes to mind: Mannerism. The superb Baroque sense for the appropriateness of ornament, however extravagant, has gone.

PROTESTANT CHURCHES IN GERMANY. Beginning as simple preaching churches, the Protestant churches of the eighteenth century nevertheless share some of the brightness of Late German Baroque. Their mood extends from Classic restraint (ill. 221) to an almost unchecked exuberance of form (ill. 224). The finest example of all was Georg Bähr's Frauenkirche (built 1726) in Dresden, now alas destroyed with the rest of the city. The tall dome of Gontard's Französischer Dome in Berlin (ill. 235, built 1780), is like a last gesture of the Baroque in the face of triumphant rationalism and the Classic revival.

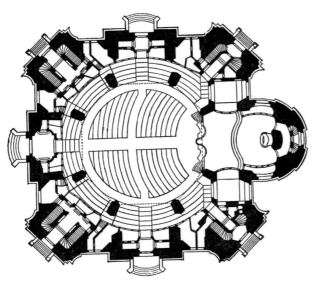

Dresden, Frauenkirche.

BELGIUM AND HOLLAND, SWEDEN, POLAND AND RUSSIA. Of the formerly united provinces of the Netherlands, Catholic Flanders developed elaborate forms, based on the Mannerist tradition. Swags and garlands are amongst the principal features of this style, whose influence spread through Flemish craftsmen - particularly wood carvers and plaster workers - to England and along the coastal region towards the Baltic. The art of Protestant Holland is far more severe (ill. 72). Decoration is chiefly confined to gables, and even a palace like the Mauritshuis in 'sGravenhage (56, below) impresses by its noble proportions rather than ornament. Country houses occasionally come closer to French examples, at least in the lay-out of the park (ill. 173), if not in splendour.

In Sweden, Protestantism proved no impenetrable barrier to the persuasive power of French Baroque. The tradition of block-like severity is still alive in the middle of the century (ill. 7, below)). Yet a mature Baroque building of the type developed in the Netherlands, could rise at the same time (ill. 56, below). Only the French Baroque forms proved suitable for the royal palaces. Stockholm was given a *cour d'honneur*, though the façade towards the water retains,

according to the wishes of the architect, Nicodemus Tessin, the serverity of Roman examples (ill. 228). The summer residence at Drottningholm also combines French and Italian features (ill. 104). Tessin's chapel of Charles XII, a centralised structure of unusual plasticity (ill. 132), forms an addition to the Gothic Riddarholms church.

Seventeenth century Poland, like Germany and Austria, gained greatly through Italian influence. When Locci had already begun the palace at Wilanow for John III Sobieski, Tylman von Gameren was still busy with as conservative a building as the Radziejowski palace at Nieborow (ill. 102, below). In the course of many changes demanded by Augustus the Strong, Wilanów became one of the most charming Baroque palaces in Eastern Europe (ill. 233, above). In its liveliness and elegance it far surpasses French and Italian examples. Church decoration displays the Polish love of ornament (ill. 129). The church at Kobylko has illusionist frescos above the elaborate cornice (ill. 167). While Catholic Poland was always in close contact with Western and Central Europe, Russia remained a world of her own. From the second half of the seventeenth century onwards Western Baroque influence begins to seep in through the Ukraine. Probably the most startling results of this mixed style is the Church of the Virgin of the Sign at Dubrovitsi (ill. 171). Sculpture, hitherto frowned upon as 'Roman', appears for the first time on an Orthodox church; the gables are covered in decoration.

The founding of St. Petersburg (to-day Leningrad) in 1703 expressed Russia's re-orientation towards the West. Le Blond, pupil of Le Nôtre, was commissioned to design Peterhof for Peter the Great. Versailles is re-created on a vast Russian scale. The middle of the century saw the beginning of two of the most important projects in the city. Their architect, Rastrelli (c. 1700-1771), the Paris-born son of an Italian sculptor, had come to Russia as a child. Extensive travel moulded his style which, though cosmopolitan, does not deny national characteristics. He was to become the first Russian architect of the Western school. His Smolny Institute (ill. 233, below) is built on a vast cruciform lay-out, with the cathedral of the Resurrection at the centre. The articulation of the long façades of the Winter Palace (begun 1754) is singularly successful (ill. 232). At Zarskoje Selo, the influence of Pöppelmann and Balthasar Neumann is particularly obvious. Yet despite points of similarity with Würzburg and Dresden, the result is unmistakably Russian.

STAIRCASES. Baroque staircases are planned far beyond practical needs. Spain had already evolved various types in the sixteenth century; in the seventeenth they occur as important features of North Italian palaces. Bartolommeo Bianco's staircase at the Jesuit College in Genoa (1630) links the hall below ground floor level with the courtyard, whence two further arms lead to the garden beyond (ill. 88). Axial lay-outs, elaborate vistas, the most surprising intersections, were eagerly aimed at. Outdoor staircases appear on churches and palaces (ills. 43, 171). The two-armed staircase of SS. Domenico e Sisto in Rome (ill. 23), built 1654, anticipates the motif of the Spanish Steps (ill. 115) by nearly seventy years. In France, where the North Italian example had been so magnificently interpreted in the Escalier des Ambassadeurs at Versailles, the interest in staircases was no longer alive in the eighteenth century. They were now considered a necessary evil, unworthy of any special attention. Not so elsewhere. Fischer von Erlach and Schlüter (ills. 97, 98) give their staircases a new Classic dignity; Lucas von Hildebrandt's staircase in the Mirabell palace (ill. 99) has had as great an influence on German Baroque architecture as Pommersfelden (ill. 190) where, for the first time in Germany, the staircase hall entirely occupies a prominent part of the building, the centre pavilion.

Balthasar Neumann's staircases are amongst the most brilliant expression of his genius. Würzburg and Brühl both have 'Kaisertreppen', so-called Imperial staircases (ills. 191, 156). Architecture, painting, plasterwork and sculpture complement each other in these superb creations of the human spirit. When his contemporaries questioned the statics of the vast hall at Würzburg (ill. 191), which had at first been planned differently, Neumann replied that one could fire a cannon in it without causing the ceiling to fall–and, indeed, it has withstood the air raids of 1945 as well as the ensuing fire storms. Amongst the many staircases of the Neumann school, one of the most charming is at Wurzach (ill. 240), another, equally late and already almost Classic, in Göttingen (ill. 236).

The Spanish Steps in Rome (ill. 115) and the pilgrims' steps at Bom Jesus do Monte near Braga, in Portugal (ill. 178) offer unparalleled scenographic effects. In Turin, where, probably earlier than elsewhere, the staircase first assumes prominence in the seventeenth century, Juvara added an extra staircase wing to the Palazzo Madama in 1718 (ill. 89). But all staircases are surpassed in the Palazzo Reale at Caserta, near Naples (ill. 194) where, as late as 1752, Baroque mastery of space has obviously lost none of its vigour.

BAROQUE LIBRARIES. Baroque libraries throughout partake of the splendour of the Baroque interior. In the Benedictine abbey at Metten (ill. 134), powerful Atlantes carry the low ceiling. The following years see a gradual loosening and brightening up. One of the last Baroque convents, Schüssenried (built 1754), has a gallery with a graceful parapet, the book-cases are carved with rocaille decoration (ill. 137). At Coimbra in Portugal the university library (ill. 138) was laid out in 1717 as a princely succession of rooms. But the finest of all eighteenth-century libraries was built by Fischer von Erlach as part of the Hofburg (ill. 136) in Vienna. Leibniz, the leading mathematician and philosopher of the age, praised the plan in an enthusiastic letter to the architect.

Eva-Maria Wagner

INDEX OF PLACES

Roman numerals denote mention in the text; Arabic numerals illustrations.

Ills. 42, 195 and 197 were reproduced from Georgina Masson, I t a l i a n   V i l l a s   a n d   P a l a c e s (Thames & Hudson, London; German edition by Droemersche Verlagsanstalt, Th. Knaur Nachf., Munich), by permission of the Publishers; ills. 104, below, and 169 by permission of the Patrimonie Nacional, Madrid.

Baroque vaulting. Arcading and transverse arches,
sculpture and painting unite like the parts of a vast orchestra.
Rome. Chiesa Nuova (M. Longhi the Elder, 1575—1605).
The fresco in the dome is by Pietro da Cortona (1647—51).   Foto: Jeiter

Rom. Die Kirche Il Gesù, zeitlich noch der Renaissanceperiode zugehörig, wurde wegweisend für den Kirchenbau des Barock. Oben: Fassade (Giacomo della Porta; Entwurf 1573). Rechts: Innenraum (Vignola, 1568–76). — Die Einzelteile des Baus sind nicht mehr selbständig, sondern werden zu einer Einheit neuer Art — durch Voluten und gekuppelte Pilaster bei der Fassade, durch das Dominieren von Vierungskuppel und Mittelschiff im Inneren.

Rome. Il Gesù, though still of the Renaissance, was to assume fundamental importance in the development of Baroque church architecture. Above: the façade (Giacomo della Porta, 1573). Right: the interior (Giacomo Vignola, 1568–76). — The separate parts are no longer independent. On the façade, unity is achieved through scrolls and coupled pilasters, in the interior through the predominance of the dome and the nave.

2

Jeiter

Rom. Die Brunnen, lebensvolle Mittelpunkte im Stadtbild, spiegeln die Ablösung der Stile. Oben: Noch manieristisch-verspielt
der Schildkrötenbrunnen (della Porta und Landini, 1585). Rechts: Acqua Felice (Fontana, 1585),
frühbarock-pompös nach Art antiker Triumphbogen, mit überbetonter Erbauungsinschrift.

Rome. Fountains. Above: Fontana delle Tartarughe (della Porta and Landini, 1585). Still playful and Mannerist. Right: Acqua Felice (Fontana, 1585).
An Early Baroque monument in the manner of a triumphal arch, with over-emphasis on the inscription.

4

Busch

Busch

Außerhalb Roms führt der Weg zum Frühbarock vielfach über eine nüchtern-klare Großformigkeit, welche die überladenen Zierformen des Manierismus ablöst.
Links: *Augsburg*. Rathausfront (Elias Holl, 1610—20).
Rechts oben: *Kloster Seckau, Steiermark* (1619—37).
Unten: *Schloß Skokloster bei Stockholm* (1646—68).

Outside Italy, the transition from Mannerist elaboration to the Early Baroque frequently takes the form of severe simplicity.
Left: *Augsburg*. Town hall (Elias Holl, 1610—20).
Right, above: the convent at *Seckau, Styria* (1619—37).
Below: *Skokloster, near Stockholm*. The Palace (1646—68).

Schneiders

Frühbarock im Norden. *Augsburg.* Zeughaus (Elias Holl, 1602—07). Voluten, betonte Gesimse und aufgesprengte Giebel sind nicht mehr bloße Flächenzier, sondern stehen im Dienste einer bewegten Plastizität des Baukörpers.

Early Baroque in the North. *Augsburg.* Zeughaus (the former city armoury, Elias Holl, 1602—07). Scrolls, cornices, and broken pediments, no longer purely decorative elements, stand in the service of dynamism and greater plasticity.

Jeiter

Frühbarock in *Rom*. S. Susanna (Maderna, 1595—1603). Weniger dynamisch, doch harmonischer als im Norden wird auch hier die Mitte stärker betont: durch Verdoppelung der Halbsäulen und Pilaster.

Early Baroque in *Rome*. S. Susanna (Maderna, 1595—1603). Less dynamic, though more harmonious than in the north. The same central emphasis, here through coupled half-columns and pilasters.

Die Illusion der durch Malerei zum Himmel geöffneten Decke, ein Lieblingsmotiv des Barock, ist bereits in der Renaissancezeit vorgebildet.
Oben: *Mantua*. Herzogschloß. Deckenmalerei des Brautzimmers (Mantegna; 1474 vollendet).
Rechts: *Parma*. S. Giovanni. Kuppelfresko „Himmelfahrt Christi" (Correggio, 1520—24).

The illusion of a ceiling opened to the sky, a favourite Baroque motif, anticipated in Renaissance art.
Above: *Mantua*. Castello dei Gonzaga. Mantegna's ceiling frescos in the Camera degli Sposi (finished 1474).
Right: *Parma*. S. Giovanni. The Ascension (Correggio, 1520—24), from the dome.

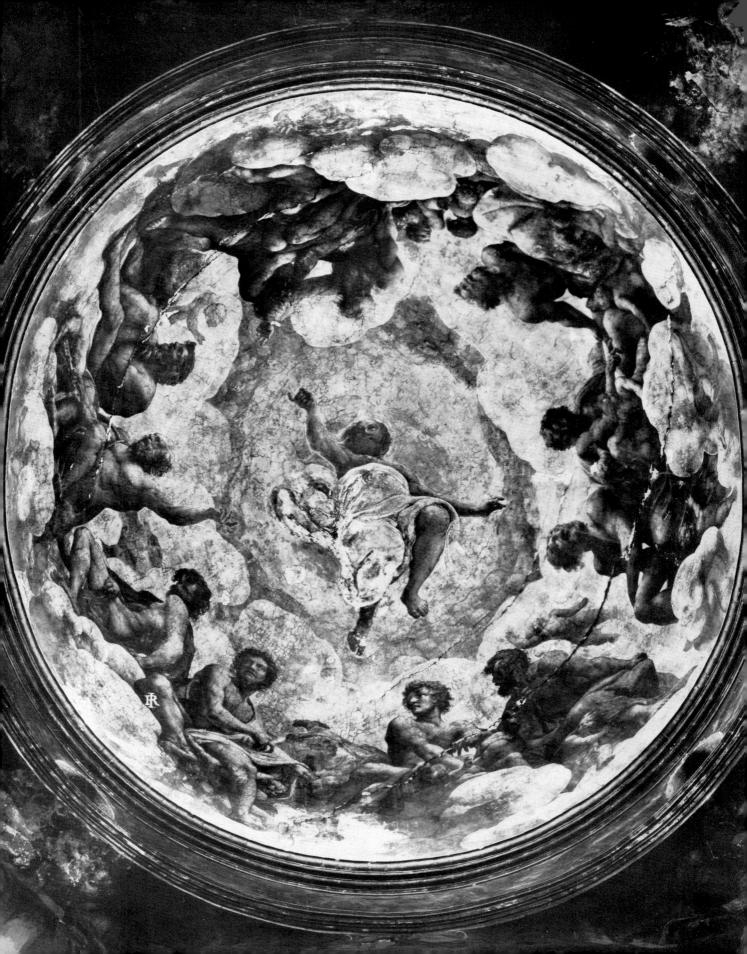

Salzburg. Dom (Solari, 1614—28). Dem Beispiel von Il Gesù folgend, mündet das dunklere Langhaus im lichterfüllten Kuppelraum. Frühes Beispiel italienischer Barockanlage im deutschen Kunstgebiet.

Salzburg. Cathedral (Solari, 1614—28). Following the plan of Il Gesù, the darker nave leads into the light-filled crossing under the dome. An early example of an Italian Baroque plan north of the Alps.

Rom. S. Agnese in Piazza Navona (Rainaldi; beg. 1645). Im reifen Barock durchziehen gewaltige Kraftströme den Baukörper. Gemeinsam treiben sie die steile Zentralkuppel empor.

Rome. S. Agnese in Piazza Navona (Rainaldi; begun 1645). In the mature Baroque, the whole composition is permeated by a stream of forces, here culminating in the tall central dome.

13

MAS

Kersting

Jeiter

Die Palastbauten des frühen Barock entwickeln sich in fast unmerklichem Übergang aus Vorbildern der Renaissance und des Manierismus.
Links oben: *Granada*. Audiencia (Navarro und Hernández, 1584–87). Unten: *London*. Banqueting Hall (Inigo Jones, 1619).
Oben: *Rom*. Palazzo Barberini (Maderna und Borromini 1625–33; Bernini bis 1663).

Baroque palace architecture develops in almost unnoticeable transition from Renaissance and Mannerism.
Left, above: *Granada*. Audiencia (Navarro and Hernández, 1584–87). Below: *London*. Banqueting Hall (Inigo Jones, 1619).
Above: *Rome*. Palazzo Barberini (Maderna and Borromini 1625–33; Bernini 1663).

Die enge Kuppelung zweier Säulen, ein Vermächtnis des Manierismus (Michelangelo) an den Barock.
Links oben: *Mailand*. Palazzo di Brera (Entw. Ricchini; beg. 1651).
Unten: *Prag*. Loggia des Palais Waldstein (Spezza, 1621–28). Oben: *Paris*. S. Gervais (de Brosse, 1616–21).

Close-coupled pillars, a legacy of Mannerism (Michelangelo).
Left, above: *Milan*. Palazzo di Brera (designed by Ricchini, begun 1651). Below: *Prague*. Loggia from the Palais Waldstein (Spezza, 1621–28).
Above: *Paris*. S. Gervais (de Brosse, 1616–21).

17

v. Matt

18

Jeiter

Rom. Kirchen als beherrschende Blickpunkte barocker Platzgestaltung. Oben: Die beiden Kuppelkirchen S. Maria in Monte Santo (links) und S. Maria dei Miracoli, Piazza del Popolo, als triumphale Eingangspforte zum päpstlichen Rom. (Rainaldi, Fontana, Bernini; 1662–78). Links: Die eingekurvte Fassade von S. Agnese (Borromini, 1652–57) an der langgestreckten Piazza Navona.

Rome. Churches as focal points of the Baroque piazza. Above: S. Maria in Monte Santo (left) and S. Maria dei Miracoli, on the Piazza del Popolo, form a triumphal gateway to papal Rome (Rainaldi, Fontana, Bernini; 1662–78). Left: the curved front of S. Agnese in Agone (Borromini, 1652–57) on the Piazza Navona.

Rom. Plastische Kraft, Pathos und Formenfülle: römischer Hochbarock. Oben: S. Pietro in Montorio (Bernini, 1636).
Rechts: Die dynamisch schwingende Front von S. Agnese (Borromini, 1652–55), davor der dramatisch bewegte Flüssebrunnen (Bernini, 1651).

Rome. The exuberance of Roman High Baroque. Above: S. Pietro in Montorio (Bernini, 1636).
Right: another view of Borromini's S. Agnese in Agone, with Bernini's Fontana dei Fiumi (1651).

Jeiter

Rom. Zwei Kirchenfassaden als charakteristische Beispiele von vielen: Kräftiges Gurtgesims, Betonung der Mitte durch Säulen und Pilaster, Nischen mit Figuren oder Reliefs.
Links: SS. Martina e Luca am Forum Romanum (Pietro da Cortona, 1635) mit reichem Schmuck der Kuppel.
Rechts: SS. Domenico e Sisto (Vincenzo della Greca, 1630).

Rome. Two characteristic Baroque church façades. Wide cornices, emphasis on a central axis through columns and pilasters, niches with figures or reliefs.
Left: SS. Martina e Luca on the Forum Romanum (Pietro da Cortona, 1635), with a lavishly decorated dome.
Right: SS. Domenico e Sisto (Vincenzo della Greca, 1630).

Rom. S. Agnese, innen (Rainaldi, beg. 1645). Einer der vier Pfeiler, die die Kuppel tragen. Sie sind schräg zum runden Zentralraum gestellt und in kühnen Bögen für Altäre geöffnet.

Rome. S. Agnese in Agone. Interior (Rainaldi, begun 1645). One of the four piers supporting the dome. They are placed diagonally and open into arched recesses for altars.

24

Rom. Die Scala Regia (1663–66) im Vatikan. Mit der virtuosen Anwendung perspektivischer Kunstgriffe des Barocktheaters verwandelt Bernini einen engen Schacht in den glanzvollen Aufgang zum Vatikanischen Palast.

Rome. The Scala Regia (1663–66) in the Vatican. Through his mastery of all the illusionist devices of the Baroque theatre, Bernini transforms a narrow passage into the splendid approach to the Vatican Palace.

Rom. Petersplatz. Zur Kuppel der Peterskirche (Michelangelo, Entw. 1557) und ihrer Fassade (Maderna, 1607—12) läßt Bernini einen Kolonnadenhof (1656—67) hinführen, der durch perspektivische Kunstgriffe noch größer erscheint.

Rome. The Piazza of St. Peter's. To Michelangelo's dome (designed 1557) and Maderna's façade (1607—12), Bernini adds a vast colonnaded piazza (1656—67), made to appear even bigger through his brilliant handling of perspective.

Rom. Peterskirche. Baldachin über dem Hochaltar (1625—33). Grundgedanke Berninis: Nur geschwungene Kolossalformen können sich neben der vertikalen Wucht der Pfeiler behaupten.

Rome. St. Peter's. Bernini's Baldacchino above the High Altar (1625—33).

Rom. Peterskirche. Machtvolle Verbindung von Renaissance und Barock — in der von Michelangelo entworfenen Kuppel mit der giebelgekrönten Säulenfassade des vorgesetzten Langhauses (Maderna, 1607–12).

Rome. St. Peter's. Renaissance and Baroque meet: Michelangelo's dome and Maderna's façade (1607–12).

Kersting

London. St. Pauls-Kathedrale (Sir Christopher Wren, 1675–1710). Lange Zeiten hindurch und bis zum reformierten England hin wirkt das römische Vorbild.

London. St. Paul's Cathedral (Sir Christopher Wren, 1675–1710). The tradition of St. Peter's lives on throughout the centuries, even in Protestant countries.

Kersting

Giraudon

Auch die Säulenform des Baldachins von St. Peter in Rom findet Nachfolge in der Barockkunst der anderen Länder.
Oben: *Oxford*. St. Mary's. Südportal (1627). Rechts: *Paris*. Val-de-Grâce. Hochaltar (G. Leduc, nach 1654) der Klosterkapelle.

The legacy of the Baldacchino of St. Peter's. Above: *Oxford*. St. Mary's. South portal (1627).
Right: *Paris*. Val-de-Grâce. High Altar (G. Leduc, after 1654) of the convent chapel.

Jeiter

Rom. Im Innenraum wie in der Freiarchitektur erhalten die großen Säulenordnungen durch Bernini ein neues Pathos.
Links: Palazzo Barberini. Die Ovaltreppe im Erdgeschoß (1625–33, vollendet 1663). Oben: Detail der Kolonnaden von St. Peter (1656–67).

Rome. Everywhere the great orders are given a new meaning by Bernini. Left: Palazzo Barberini. The oval staircase (1625–33, completed 1663).
Above: detail from the colonnade of St. Peter's (1656–67).

Jeiter

Rom. S. Andrea al Quirinale (Bernini 1678). Dem ovalen Kirchenraum entspricht im Westen ein Portalvorbau mit diademähnlicher Bekrönung. Strenge Formen von antikischer Hoheit — ein Vermächtnis des reifen Bernini.

Rome. S. Andrea al Quirinale (Bernini, 1678). Bernini's maturest work, designed entirely by him.

34

Jeiter

Rom. S. Maria della Pace (Pietro da Cortona, 1656—57). Die Mitte wird ein plastisch zur Straße vortretender Körper,
die Seitenachsen ergeben eine in reicher Brechung zurückweichende Kulisse.

Rome. S. Maria della Pace (Pietro da Cortona, 1656—57). Projecting centre block with receding wings.

35

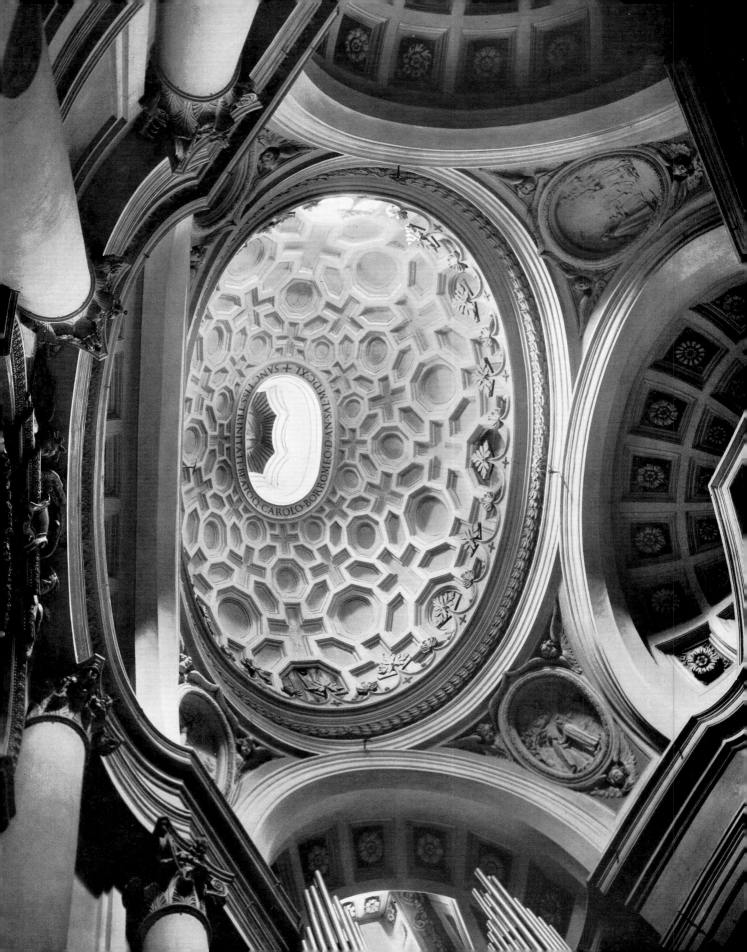

Kersting

Jeiter

Auf klassisch ruhige Formen folgen komplizierte Kuppelbildungen.
Links: *Rom.* S. Carlo alle quattro Fontane (Borromini, 1638–40). Kuppel über ovalem Kirchenraum.
Oben: *Turin.* S. Lorenzo (beg. 1634, Guarini ab 1666). Kuppelbau in Weiterführung mittelalterlicher Rippenkonstruktion.

Classic calm and simplicity is succeeded by greater elaboration. Left: *Rome.* S. Carlo alle quattro Fontane (Borromini, 1638–40). A dome over an oblong plan.
Above: *Turin.* S. Lorenzo (begun 1634, completed by Guarini after 1666). A Baroque version of medieval rib vaulting.

37

Rom. S. Carlo alle quattro Fontane (Borromini, 1667). Die italienische Architektur
wendet sich dynamischer Bewegtheit mit Kurven und Schwingungen zu.

Rome. S. Carlo alle quattro Fontane (Borromini, 1667). Italian architecture
develops livelier movement and undulating lines.

Kersting

Turin. S. Lorenzo (beg. 1634; unter Guarini ab 1666). Altarwand. Ein reiches System einander durchdringender
Bau- und Raumteile — Quell der Anregungen für den nordischen Spätbarock.

Turin. S. Lorenzo (begun 1634; completed by Guarini after 1666). Interior. An elaborate system
of interpenetration and an important influence on Late Northern Baroque.

Jeiter

Rom. S. Ivo (1642—60) — eine der eigenwilligsten Schöpfungen Borrominis. Die Fassade (links) fängt den Hof mit den Segmentbogen des fünfachsigen Portalbaus auf. Energische Gegenschwünge der sechsteiligen Kuppel, die sich innen leicht und elegant wie ein geblähtes Segel erhebt (oben).

Rome. S. Ivo (1642—60). One of Borromini's most startling creations. Left: the façade. Above: the sexpartite dome, which rises above the interior like a wind-filled sail.

41

Stursberg

Venedig. Palazzo Pesaro (Longhena, ab 1679). Zum herkömmlichen System der venezianischen Palazzi fügt der Barock das mächtigere Gesamtvolumen, die lebhaftere Rustizierung und die Zwillingsstellung der Säulen.

Venice. Palazzo Pesaro (Longhena, from 1679).
Livelier rustication, twin columns and greater emphasis on volume, the Baroque contribution to Venetian palace architecture.

Venedig. Santa Maria della Salute (Longhena, beg. 1631). Reiche Treppensockel zum Anlegen der Gondeln, gespannte Kraft der Voluten, majestätische Kuppel über achtseitigem Zentralraum.

Venice. Santa Maria della Salute (Longhena, begun 1631). Steps as landing stages, scrolled buttresses and a majestic round dome above an octagonal plan.

Versailles. Cour de Marbre (de Brosse, Le Vau, Hardouin-Mansart; 1624–79).
Das System der oberitalienischen Villa, in die Dimensionen des französischen Absolutismus übersetzt.

Versailles. Cour de Marbre (de Brosse, Le Vau and Hardouin-Mansart, 1624–79). The North Italian villa, translated into the language of French absolutism.

44

Roubier

Blois. Das Renaissanceschloß erhält durch Mansart einen barocken Ehrenhof (1635–
Das Mittelfenster tritt als Herzstück hervor und bildet mit Kartusche und Figuren der Dachzone eine kraftvolle Einh

Blois. Mansart adds a Baroque *cour d'honneur* (1635–38) to the Renaissance château. Emphasis on a central a

Schmidt-Glassner

Die Innenräume französischer Schlösser werden in der 1. Hälfte des 17. Jh. von den prunkvollen Dekorationen beherrscht, die der römische Barock entwickelt hatte. Auch Anklänge an die Renaissance leben weiter. Links: *Paris*. Hôtel Lambert, Galérie d'Hercule (Le Vau, 1640; Ausstattung Lebrun und Le Sueur). Oben: *Cheverny*. Appartement du Roi (vor 1634).

The influence of the Roman Baroque on the aristocratic French interior of the first half of the seventeenth century. The Renaissance tradition is still far from extinct. Left: *Paris*. Hôtel Lambert, Galérie d'Hercule (Le Vau, 1640; the decoration by Lebrun and Le Sueur). Above: *Cheverny*. Appartement du Roi (before 1634).

47

Versailles. Das Schloß
(beg. 1624 von de Brosse;
Umbau von Le Vau, beg. 1668;
Neugestaltung von Hardouin-
Mansart, beg. 1679).
Vorbild höfischer Repräsentation
für alle Generationen
des späteren Barock.
Strahlenförmig
gehen drei Straßen,
die mittlere nach Paris,
vom Zentralpunkt
der Anlage aus —
dem Schlafgemach
des Sonnenkönigs.

Versailles. Begun by de Brosse,
1624; re-modelled by Le Vau,
from 1668; completed by
Hardouin-Mansart, after 1679.
The archetype of the royal palace
throughout the Baroque.
Three roads—the middle
one leading to Paris—
radiate from the centre
of the whole composition,
the bedroom of the *roi soleil.*

Versailles. Die Spiegelgalerie (Hardouin-Mansart, beg. 1678; Dekoration von Lebrun). Majestätisch die Abmessungen (72 x 10 x 13 m).
Im Wechsel von Pilastern und festlichen Rundbogen, in dem mit Festons geschmückten Gesims und der Tonnenwölbung ein einheitliches Gesamtkunstwerk.

Versailles. The Galérie des Glaces (Hardouin-Mansart, begun 1678; decorated by Lebrun).
Truly regal proportions (240 ft. x 34 ft. x 43 ft.) and perfect balance of all its parts.

E. Müller

Versailles. Schloßkapelle (Hardouin-Mansart, 1699–1710). Über den Pfeilerarkaden des Erdgeschosses ein Säulenumgang mit ruhigem Gurtgesims. Akademisch kühle Klarheit – die Bewegtheit des römischen Spätbarock wird nicht erstrebt.

Versailles. The chapel (Hardouin-Mansart, 1699–1710). Above the arcades of the ground floor a colonnade with a simple entablature. Cool and scholarly clarity, without any of the dynamism of Roman Late Baroque.

Die klassische Form der Schloßanlage mit Pavillons und Ehrenhof entwickelt sich in Frankreich. Oben: *Château de Luynes bei Dampierre*
(Hardouin-Mansart, 1675–83). Vor dem flacheren Ehrenhof der Haupttrakte zwei abgesetzte Seitenflügel. Rechts oben: *Cheverny*. Schloß, Parkseite
(Boyer, voll. 1634). Besonders zart und vornehm in der Dekoration, mit wechselnder Dachbildung. Unten: *Lyon*. Rathaus (Maupin 1646–72;
Umgestaltung 1702 durch Hardouin-Mansart). Vor Kuppeltürmen die dreitorige Einfahrt in den Ehrenhof.

The development of the château with *cour d'honneur* is a specifically French contribution to the Baroque. Above: *Château de Luynes near Dampierre*
(Hardouin-Mansart, 1675–83). Central block with two flanking wings. Right, above: *Cheverny*. Garden front (Boyer, 1634).
Of great elegance and restraint in the decoration with changing roof forms. Below: *Lyons*. Town hall
(Maupin 1646–72; re-modelled 1702 by Hardouin-Mansart). In front of the towers the entrance to the *cour d'honneur*.

52

Cash

Flämische und niederländische Anregungen und Nachklänge des Tudorstils prägen die englische Baukunst im frühen 17. Jh.
Oben: *Wilton House bei Salisbury*. Der „Double Cube Room", für die Familienbildnisse von van Dyck entworfen,
zeigt neben barocken Einzelheiten starke klassizistische Tendenz (Inigo Jones und John Webb, um 1649; Deckenmalerei von Edward Pierce d. Ä.).
Rechts: *London*. Dutch House in Kew Gardens (1631). Eines der letzten Giebelhäuser dieses Stils,
bevor sich der Einfluß Palladios mit Inigo Jones endgültig durchsetzt.

English architecture of the early seventeenth century is largely determined by Dutch and Flemish influence, with strong Tudor elements.
Above: *Wilton House near Salisbury*. The Double Cube Room, designed for van Dyck's family portraits, shows strong Classic tendencies,
despite Baroque detail (Inigo Jones and John Webb, c. 1649; the ceiling by Edward Pierce the Elder).
Right: *London*. The Dutch House at Kew Gardens (1631). One of the last gabled houses in this style,
before the complete triumph of Palladianism through Inigo Jones.

54

Monumenten-
zorg

Lennert
af Petersen

Jeiter

Der flämische Barock beläßt den Fassaden ihre Ruhe. Behäbige Proportionen, Girlanden und Gehänge als Flächenschmuck. Links oben: *'s Gravenhage.* Mauritshuis (J. von Campen, P. Post 1633–44; 1704–18 erneuert).
Unten: *Stockholm.* Ritterhaus (Jean de la Vallée, H. W. u. J. Vingboons, 1641–74).

In Flanders, the Baroque façade remains calm, with comfortable proportions and a love for swags and garlands. Left, above: *'s Gravenhage.* The Mauritshuis (J. van Campen, P. Post 1633–44, re-modelled 1704–18).
Below: *Stockholm.* Riddarhuset (Jean de la Vallée, H. W. and J. Vingboons, 1641–74).

Averbode, Flandern. Klosterkirche (J. van den Eynde, 1664–1701). Weiterleben gotischen Höhendrangs im flandrischen Barock.

Averbode, Flanders. Convent church (J. van den Eynde, 1664–1701). Gothic striving for height in the Flemish Baroque.

Editions S. L.

Avignon. Palais de la Monnaie (1610–21). Auch in Frankreich
erscheint im Frühbarock die spartanisch glatte Fassade,
aus dem Renaissance-Palazzo entwickelt,
welcher der schwere Stuck nur gleichsam aufgelegt ist.

Avignon. Palais de la Monnaie (1610–21).
A French example of the almost Spartan Early Baroque façade,
not unlike a Renaissance palace, with super-imposed heavy stucco decoration.

Paris. Eglise des Filles de l'Assomption
(Entw. Errard de Chéret; 1670–76).
Kuppel und Säulenvorhalle nach dem Vorbild von St. Peter kombiniert.
Die Bauglieder erscheinen jedoch flächiger, die Kuppel von erdrückender Wucht.

Paris. Eglise des Filles de l'Assomption (Errard de Chéret; 1670–76).
Based on St. Peter's, Rome. The detail more two-dimensional,
the dome of an almost overwhelming power.

59

Paris. Val-de-Grâce (beg. v. Mansart, fortgeführt v. Lemercier, 1645—65). Der mit Säulenpaaren und Dreiecksgiebel
dem Baukörper weit vorgestellte Portikus ist das Merkmal zahlreicher französischer Barockkirchen.

Paris. Val-de-Grâce (begun by Mansart, completed by Lemercier, 1645—65).
The gabled porch with its coupled pillars is characteristic of many French Baroque churches.

60

Giraudon

Paris. S. Sulpice (Le Vau, beg. 1655). In den hohen Stichkappen des Gewölbes und in der Chorbildung klingt gotisches Raumgefühl nach. Die Gesimse ohne den italienischen Stuckdekor.

Paris. S. Sulpice (begun by Le Vau, 1655). A return to the Gothic plan and Gothic feeling for space. The entablatures without Italian stucco decoration.

Paris. Invalidendom (Hardouin-Mansart, 1677-1706). Weltlich-feierliche Formensprache.
Links: Die Kolossalsäulen der Fassade bilden, dreifach vorgetreppt, ein majestätisches Doppelportal.
Oben: Das säkularisierte Gepräge des Zentralraums erfuhr durch den Einbau des Mausoleums für Napoleon eine nachdrückliche Bestätigung.

Paris. The Dome of the Invalids (Hardouin-Mansart, 1677–1706). Left: the colossal orders of the façade form an impressive two-storied portico.
Above: the secular character of the interior is given further emphasis by Napoleon's mausoleum.

Lahaye

Maastricht, Holland. Rathaus (1658–64). In der Nachfolge der palladianischen Spätrenaissance gestaltet Pieter Post den Kuppelraum in abgewogener, kühler Klassizität.

Maastricht, Holland. Town Hall (1658–64). Pieter Post's restrained and balanced interior in the tradition of the Palladian Late Renaissance.

Kersting

65

Abingdon, Berkshire. Rathaus (Chr. Kempster, um 1677). Zusammenwirken von oberitalienischen
und französischen Anregungen in der Periode der „Restoration".
Abingdon, Berks. Town Hall (Christopher Kempster, c. 1677). Traces of North Italian and French influence in the Restoration style.

Maré

In der Architektur der Barockzeit in Frankreich und insbesondere in England überwiegt eine akademisch-kühle Tendenz, die zum Klassizismus führt.
Oben: *Chelsea, London.* Royal Hospital (Wren, 1682–89). Mittelrisalit des Seitenflügels. Rechts oben: *Paris.* Louvre, Ostfassade (Perrault, 1667–70).
Unten: *Paris.* Hôtel des Invalides, Hoffassade (Bruant, 1671–74).

In France, and particularly England, Classic-academic trends predominate. Above: *London.* Royal Hospital, Chelsea (Sir Christopher Wren, 1682–89).
One of the wings. Right, above: *Paris.* Louvre. East elevation (Perrault, 1667–70). Below: *Paris.* Hôtel des Invalides. Courtyard (Bruant, 1671–74).

Jack Scheerboom

Ullstein-Lehnartz

Lüden/Kersting

Weithin sichtbare, wechselnd gestaltete Helme kennzeichnen die Barocktürme
der protestantischen Küstenstädte. Links außen: *Hamburg*. Katharinenkirche
(Turm von P. Marquardt, 1657—59). Links: *London*. St. Bride's, Fleet Street (1702—03).

Prominent and elaborate lanterns, a feature of the Protestant Baroque
churches of the coast. Extreme left: *Hamburg*. Katharinenkirche (the tower
by P. Marquardt, 1657—59). Left: *London*. St. Bride's, Fleet Street (1702—03).

London. St. Stephen, Walbrook (Wren, 1672—87).
Zentralkuppel auf acht Arkaden
über freigestellten Säulen. Variation eines Guarini-Motivs.

London. St. Stephen, Walbrook (Sir Christopher Wren, 1672—87).
A central dome over eight arcades
supported by free columns. Variation of a Guarini motif.

Der britische Barock wurde entscheidend von oberitalienischer Palastarchitektur beeinflußt. Oben: *London*. Greenwich Hospital.
Im Vordergrund Queen's House (Inigo Jones, 1616—35; Kolonnaden 19. Jh.). Unten: *Cambridge*. Trinity College, Bibliothek (Wren, 1676—84).

The influence of Northern Italy, particularly Palladio and Longhena, in England. Above: *London*. Greenwich Hospital, now the Royal Naval College.
In the foreground, the Queen's House (Inigo Jones, 1616—35; the colonnades 19th ct.). Below: Trinity College, *Cambridge*. The Library (Wren, 1676—84).

Maré

London. Eine der beiden Kuppeln des Greenwich Hospital, jetzt Royal Naval College (Wren, nach 1700). Sie geben mit ihren kraftvoll gewölbten Gurtgesimsen über den Eckrisaliten des Tambours weit mehr barocke Dynamik als die flächigen Fassaden.

London. Greenwich Hospital (now the Royal Naval College). One of the two domes (Sir Christopher Wren, after 1700).

Roubier

Jeiter

Patrizierhäuser in *Amsterdam* an der Herengracht (links) und in *Brüssel* am Marktplatz (oben, nach 1697).
Die bürgerliche Baukunst des Nordens hält — bei aller Vielfalt der neuen Dekoration — meist an der schmalen Hausform des Mittelalters fest.
Der Stil des kalvinistischen Holland ist strenger als der des katholischen Belgien.

Rich merchants' houses on the Herengracht in *Amsterdam* (left) and on the Grand'Place, *Brussels* (after 1697).
Despite the almost infinite variety of its decoration, the private house in the North generally retains its narrow medieval plan.
In Calvinist Holland, the style is more severe than in Catholic Belgium.

In den Schöpfungen des Kunsthandwerks leben — durch Renaissance und Manierismus hindurch — mittelalterliche Traditionen fort, die sich nun mit Elementen des Barock mischen. Oben: *Wettingen, Schweiz*. Klosterkirche, Chorgestühl (1601—04; Bekrönung später).
Rechts: *Schönkirchen bei Kiel*. Pfarrkirche, Altar (Hans Gudeverdt d. J., 1653).

In the crafts, medieval traditions, having survived throughout the Renaissance and Mannerism, continue into the Baroque.
Above: *Wettingen, Switzerland*. Convent church. Choir stalls (1601—04, the canopies later).
Right: *Schönkirchen, near Kiel*. Parish church. Altar (Hans Gudeverdt the Younger, 1653).

Überquellender Reichtum der Dekoration und theatralischer Ausdruck des Barock führen zur Volkstümlichkeit dieses Stils auch in südlichen Ländern.
Oben: *Belec, Jugoslawien*. Dorfkirche. Unbefangenes Überladen durch Ausstattung.
Rechts: *Toledo, Spanien*. Kathedrale. Das „Trasparente" (Narciso Tomé, 1721–32) im Chorumgang. Kunstvolle Verschmelzung von Plastik und Architektur.

Southern versions of the Baroque. Above: *Belec, Yugoslavia*. Parish church. Unrestrained exuberance in the decoration.
Right: *Toledo, Spain*. Cathedral. The "Trasparente" (Narciso Tomé, 1721–32) in the ambulatory. Skilful merging of sculpture and architecture.

Roubier

Wuchernder Schmucktrieb verbindet Elemente verschiedener Herkunft in südlichen Kirchenfronten.
Links: *Lecce, Apulien.* S. Croce (1582–1644). Erinnerungen an Mittelalter und Renaissance verbinden sich mit sizilianisch-spanischem Barock.
Oben: *Venedig.* S. Moïsè (A. Tremignan, 1668). Auf der flachen Schauseite üppige Girlanden und manieristisch gebänderte Halbsäulen.

Southern church façades. Left: *Lecce, Apulia.* S. Croce (1582–1644). A synthesis of Medieval and Renaissance elements with Sicilian-Spanish Baroque.
Above: *Venice.* S. Moïsè (A. Tremignan, 1668). Garlands and Mannerist banded half columns.

Murcia, Südspanien. Kathedrale (Jaime Bort y Melià, beg. 1737). Aufgesprengte Fassade mit auseinandergebogenen Giebeln, tief gekurvten Wänden und flackerndem Dekor. Ein Hauptwerk des spanischen Spätbarock.

Murcia, Southern Spain. Cathedral (Jaime Bort y Melià, begun 1737). One of the principal works of Spanish Late Baroque.

80

Armao

Ragusa Ibla, Sizilien. S. Giorgio (geweiht 1738). Unter der Herrschaft spanischer Vizekönige vermischen sich auf der Insel spanische und italienische Formen. Dynamik der eingeschwungenen Front, Biegsamkeit und Eleganz der Komposition.

Ragusa Ibla, Sicily. S. Giorgio (consecrated 1738). Mingling of Spanish and Italian forms.

81

Flächen, die ganz von Ornament übersponnen sind, kennzeichnen alle Stilphasen der spanischen Kunst. Oben: *Sevilla*. Santa Maria la Blanca. Gewölbe und Kuppel scheinen in den Wirbeln spiraliger Stuckdekoration wild bewegt (P. und M. de Borja, 1659). Rechts: *Granada*. Sakristei der Kartause (L. de Arevalo, 1727–64). Anregungen exotischer Kunst geben dem spanischen Barock eine Beimischung fremdartiger Phantastik.

Areas covered by ornament were at all times characteristic of Spanish art. Above: *Seville*. Santa Maria la Blanca. A veritable riot of plasterwork (P. and M. de Borja, 1659). Right: *Granada*. Sacristy of the Carthusian convent (L. de Arevalo, 1727–64). Elements of exotic art give Spanish Baroque architecture at times an almost bizarre quality.

Echagüe

Santiago de Compostela, Spanien. Die barocke Turmfront der gotischen Kathedrale ergibt durch ständig wechselnde Gliederung und überreichen Schmuck eine bewegte Kulisse (Casas y Novoa, 1738—49).

Santiago de Compostela, Spain. The Baroque tower of the Gothic cathedral (Casas y Novoa, 1738—49).

Chihuahua, Mexiko. Kathedrale (1738–41). Die Bauten im überseeischen Kolonialreich übernehmen mit den Elementen des spanischen Kirchenbaus auch die aufgesetzten Säulengruppen.

Chihuahua, Mexico. Cathedral (1738–41). The principles of Spanish church architecture applied to the buildings of Spain's overseas possessions.

Elfer-Mauritius

In Mittel- und Südamerika werden europäische Motive völlig im Sinn indianischen Kunstempfindens verwendet. In wucherndem Blattwerk verlieren sich die tektonischen Elemente. Links: *Arequipa, Peru*. Oben: *S. Cristobal de las Casas, Mexiko* (um 1700).

In Central and South America, European motifs are interpreted in an entirely Indian spirit. Structural elements are completely lost in a wealth of decoration. Left: *Arequipa, Peru*. Above: *S. Cristobal de las Casas, Mexico* (c. 1700).

Monumentale Treppenhäuser — eine Neuschöpfung des Barock — werden zu einem bestimmenden Bestandteil der Palastarchitektur, insbesondere in
Oberitalien und Deutschland. Oben: *Genua*. Jesuitenkolleg, jetzt Universität (Bartolomeo Bianco, 1630).
Rechts: *Turin*. Palazzo Madama (Juvara, 1718—21).

Monumental staircases — a creation of the Baroque — play a decisive part in Baroque palace architecture, particularly in Northern Italy and Germany.
Above: *Genoa*. Jesuit College, now the University (Bartolomeo Bianco, 1630). Right: *Turin*. Palazzo Madama (Juvara, 1718—21).

Neumeister

Schmidt-Glassner

In Deutschland entstehen nach dem Einschnitt des Dreißigjährigen Krieges die großen Kuppelkirchen nach römischen Vorbildern und zunächst durch italienische Architekten. Links: *Passau*. Dom (Luragho 1668; Stuck von Carlone und d'Aglio, 1678—86). Oben: *München*. Theatinerkirche (beg. von Barella 1663; fortgef. von Zuccali; Stuck 1672—75; Fassade 1765—68 von Cuvilliés).

After the Thirty Years' War, domed churches on the Roman model, at first by Italian architects, were built throughout Germany. Left: *Passau*. Cathedral (Luragho, 1668; plasterwork by Carlone and d'Aglio, 1678—86). Above: *Munich*. Theatinerkirche (begun by Barella 1663; continued by Zuccali; plasterwork 1672—75; façade by Cuvilliés).

91

SPECIES TIBI CHRISTIANE DATVR.

Neumeister

Frodl-Kraft

St. Florian, Oberösterreich. Stiftskirche St. Florian (Carlone 1686–1708). Ein neuer Bewegungsrhythmus kündigt mit vorspringenden Emporen die Sonderentwicklung des Barock in Deutschland an.

St. Florian, Austria. Convent church (Carlone, 1686–1708). A change of rhythmic accents (projecting galleries, etc.) marks the beginning of a specifically German development of the Baroque.

Prag. St. Nikolaus auf der Kleinseite. Inneres nach Nordwesten (Christ. u. K. Ignaz Dientzenhofer, 1703–53). Der Raum ist in flutende Bewegung geraten: Weiterführung der Gedanken von Borromini und Guarini.

Prague. St. Nikolaus-Kleinseite. Interior, looking north-west (Christ. and K. Ignaz Dientzenhofer, 1703–53). The plan pulsates with movement: the logical conclusion of the principles of Borromini and Guarini.

Prag. St. Nikolaus in der Altstadt, Mittelrisalit der Fassade (K. I. Dientzenhofer, 1732—37). Im Wechsel von Höhlungen und vortretenden Säulen, Figuralplastik und Giebeln entsteht trotz flächiger Mauerführung eine kraftvoll bewegte Front.

Prague. St. Nikolaus, Altstadt (K. I. Dientzenhofer, 1732—37). Columns, sculpture and pediments introduce movement to a straight front.

Frodl Kraft

Wien. Peterskirche (Lucas von Hildebrandt, 1702—33). Auf das eng begrenzte Terrain einer C
wird eine Fassade nach römischem Vorbild (S. Agnese in Piazza Navona

Vienna. Peterskirche (Lucas von Hildebrandt, 1702—33). A façade inspired
in Piazza Navona, Rome, transferred to a setting of narrow Vie

Schmidt-Glassner

Foto Marburg

Berlin. Mit dem Schloß der preußischen Könige (1608—1707; 1950 gesprengt) ging das bedeutendste Werk Andreas Schlüters verloren.
Seine plastische Begabung verwandelte römische und französische Anregungen zu klar geordneten, dynamisch belebten Schöpfungen.
Oben: Südfront, Schlüterportal. Rechts: Treppenhaus im Ostflügel des Innenhofes.

Berlin. The former Imperial Palace (1608—1707; blown up 1950) contained Andreas Schlüter's most outstanding work.
Roman and French elements mingle in his well-ordered, rhythmic creations. Above: The main entrance. Right: Staircase in the east wing.

Frodl-Kraft

Frodl-Kraft   Das Treppenhaus wird, besonders nördlich der Alpen, ein Mittelpunkt der Repräsentation. Links: *Wien*. Gartenpalais Trautson (Fischer von Erlach, 1710).
Strenge, fast klassizistische Gliederung der Wände; nur mächtige Atlanten und Sphinxen als Schmuck.
Oben: *Salzburg*. Schloß Mirabell (L. von Hildebrandt, 1722—1726; Figuren von G. R. Donner). Die Balustrade ist zu sprühendem Ornament umgebildet.

Increasing importance of the staircase hall, particularly north of the Alps, as the focal point of representation.
Left: *Vienna*. Palais Trautson (Fischer von Erlach, 1710). Severe, almost Classic articulation of the walls.
Above: *Salzburg*. Schloß Mirabell (L. von Hildebrandt, 1722—1726; sculpture by Raphael Donner). Sparkling exuberance of the balustrade.

Chmel

Salzburg. Schloß Klesheim (Fischer von Erlach, 1700—1709). Die Eleganz
von Versailles verbindet sich mit strenger römischer Quaderung, deren Kühle
durch die geschwungene Balustrade der Rampe gemildert wird.

Salzburg. Schloss Klesheim (Fischer von Erlach, 1700—1709). The elegance
of Versailles, combined with severe Roman rustication, whose effect is
softened by the curved balustrade.

Ministry of Works

London. Chiswick House. Mittelrisalit (Lord Burlington u. W. Kent, 1729).
Über der Vierflügeltreppe ein Tempelportikus, der Palladio und dem Louvre
seine Reverenz erweist. Jede „barocke" Kurve ist vermieden.

London. Chiswick House (Lord Burlington and William Kent, 1729).
Entrance front. The portico above the four-armed staircase recalls Palladio
and the Louvre. ''Baroque'' curves have been carefully avoided.

Kersting

Wolynski

Kersting

Aufnahme barocker Einzelzüge in die Bauweise auch der ländlichen Adelssitze. Oben: *Raynham Hall, Norfolk.* Ostfront (Inigo Jones zugeschr.).
Zu holländischen Giebeln ein von Palladio angeregter Mittelrisalit. Unten: *Nieborów, Polen.* Radziejowski-Palast. Hauptfassade, Nordseite
(Tylman von Gameren, 1695—97). Rechts: *Ragley Hall, Warwickshire.* Eingangshalle (1680). Zu flächiger Gliederung eine graziöse Rocaille-Dekoration.

The gradual adoption of individual Baroque features, even in country houses. Above: *Raynham Hall, Norfolk.* East front (attributed to Inigo Jones).
Dutch gables and a pedimented Palladian centre block. Below: *Nieborów, Poland.* Radziejowski Palace. Main (north) front (Tylman von Gameren, 1695—97).
Right: *Ragley Hall, Warwickshire.* Entrance hall (1680). Rocaille decoration contrasts with the flat treatment of the walls.

PERI

Fürstliche Lustschlösser erhalten nach dem Vorbild von Versailles den Charakter weitläufiger Residenzen.
Links oben: *Drottningholm bei Stockholm.* Gartenfront (beg. von Nic. Tessin d. Ä. 1662, voll. v. Tessin d. J. 1700).
Unten: *La Granja bei Madrid* (Juvara und Sacchetti, 1735–39). Gartenfront. Oben: *Pillnitz bei Dresden.*
Bergpalais (Pöppelmann zugeschr., nach 1720). Die pagodenförmigen Dächer folgen der Vorliebe des Rokoko für Chinoiserien.

The influence of Versailles on the country houses of princes and kings. Left, above: *Drottningholm, near Stockholm.*
Garden front (begun by N. Tessin 1662, completed by his son, 1700). Below: *La Granja, near Madrid* (Juvara and Sacchetti, 1735–1739). Garden front.
Above: *Pillnitz, near Dresden.* Bergpalais (attributed to Pöppelmann, after 1720). Pagoda roofs, in keeping with the Rococo love of Chinoiserie.

105

Seaton Delaval, Northumberland. Ehrenhof (1720–29).
Sir John Vanbrugh verleiht der englischen Barockarchitektur
einen Zug von Kraft und Selbstbewußtsein.

Seaton Delaval, Northumberland. Cour d'honneur (1720–29).
Vanbrugh adds vigour and originality to English Baroque architecture.

Blenheim Palace, Oxfordshire. Südportal des Ehrenhofes (Vanbrugh, 1705–24).
Rustizierung wichtiger Bauteile, Monumentalität der Proportionen.

Blenheim Palace, Oxon. Main entrance (Sir John Vanbrugh, 1705–24).
Monumental proportions, heavy rustication
on the principal parts of the façade.

Gunther Schmidt - Bavaria

Flächigeres Relief der Fassadengliederung schon vor der Mitte des 18. Jh. Links: *Rom*. Palazzo della Consultà, Mittelrisalit (Fuga, 1732–37).
Oben: *München*. Erzbischöfliches Palais (Cuvilliés, 1733–37). Zur strengen Gliederung tritt in Deutschland oft Stuckdekoration.

A flatter, more relief-like treatment of the façade occurs already before the middle of the eighteenth century.
Left: *Rome*. Palazzo della Consultà, centre portion (Ferdinando Fuga, 1732–37).

Above: *Munich*. The Archbishop's palace (Cuvilliés, 1733–37). In Germany, stucco decoration is often used in connection with severely articulated walls.

Deutlich zeigen die großen Schloßbauten um die Mitte des 18. Jh. den Wandel vom plastischen zum breitgelagert-flächigen Bauen.
Oben: *Schloß Compiègne* (1751—88). Rechts oben: *Potsdam*. Neues Palais (Büring, Manger, Gontard 1763—69).
Unten: *Madrid*. Königliches Schloß (Juvara und Sacchetti, 1738—64).

The transition from Baroque plasticity to a more expansive and two-dimensional manner, reflected in mid-eighteenth century palace architecture.
Above: *Compiègne* (1751—88). Right, above: *Potsdam*. Neues Palais (Büring, Manger, Gontard 1763—69).
Below: *Madrid*. Royal Palace (Juvara and Sacchetti, 1738—64).

110

Baur

Jeiter

Defner

Rom. S. Maria di Loreto (Kirche links;
Antonio da Sangallo, 1507; Laterne 1592 von G. del Duca)
und S. Nome di Maria (Dérizet 1736). Daneben Trajanssäule.

Rome. S. Maria di Loreto (on the left;
Antonio da Sangallo, 1507; the lantern 1592 by G. del Duca)
and S. Nome di Maria (Dérizet, 1736), with Trajan's Column.

Wien. Karlskirche (J. B. Fischer v. Erlach, 1715—23).
Rom hat den Wiener Architekten inspiriert: antikische Giebelvorhalle,
beherrschende Kuppel, von zwei Riesensäulen und zwei Türmen flankiert.

Vienna. Karlskirche (J. B. Fischer von Erlach, 1715—23).
The inspiration of St. Peter's Classic portico and a vast dome,
flanked by two columns and two pavilions.

11

Prag. St. Nikolaus auf der Kleinseite
(Chr. u. K. I. Dientzenhofer, 1703–51; Kuppel und Turm Luragho, 1755).
Über gewundenen Altstadtstraßen mit Barockpalästen
drängen Kuppel und Turm wuchtig empor.

Prague. St. Nikolaus-Kleinseite (Chr. and K. I. Dientzenhofer, 1703–51;
dome and tower by Luragho, 1755).

Rom. Die Spanische Treppe (A. Specchi und F. de Sanctis, 1721–26)
mit Obelisk und S. Trinità dei Monti (Fassade v. G. della Porta, 1585).
Vorn: Schiffsbrunnen (Pietro Bernini, 1626).

Rome. The Piazza di Spagna (A. Specchi and F. de Sanctis, 1721–26)
with the obelisk and S. Trinità dei Monti (façade by G. della Porta, 1585).
In the foreground Pietro Bernini's fountain (1626).

114

Barocke Straßen und Plätze nördlich der Alpen. Oben: *Hirschberg, Schlesien*. Die Lauben.
Rechts oben: *Eichstätt, Franken*. Kavaliershöfe am Residenzplatz (Gabrieli, 30er Jahre des 18. Jh.).
Unten: *Prag*. Kleinseitener Ring. Adelshäuser (16.–18. Jh.).

Baroque streets and squares north of the Alps. Above: *Hirschberg, Silesia*. The "Lauben".
Right, above: *Eichstätt, Franconia*. Grace and favour houses on the Residenzplatz (Giovanni Gabrieli, 'thirties of the eighteenth century).
Below: *Prague*. The Kleinseitener Ring (sixteenth to eighteenth century).

116

Aufsberg

Deutsche Fotothek

Schneiders

Löbl

Klosteranlagen wetteifern an Pracht mit den weltlichen Residenzen der Barockzeit. Oben: *St. Florian, Oberösterreich* (Carlone und Prandtauer, 1686–1714). Unten: *Ettal, Oberbayern* (E. Zuccali und J. Schmuzer, 1710–52). Rechts: *Melk an der Donau, Österreich* (J. Prandtauer, 1702–36).

Monasteries vie in splendour with the palaces of the nobility. Above: *St. Florian, Austria* (Carlone, J. Prandtauer, 1686–1714). Below: *Ettal, Bavaria* (E. Zuccali, J. Schmuzer, 1710–52). Right: *Melk on the Danube, Austria* (J. Prandtauer, 1702–36).

Plastische Ausformung
des Mittelbaus — angeregt
vom römischen Barock
(Bernini, Borromini).
Links: *Salzburg.*
Kollegienkirche (J. B. Fischer
von Erlach, 1696).
Rechts:
Weingarten, Oberschwaben.
Westfront der Klosterkirche
(C. Moosbrugger, 1715;
Fassade: Mitarbeit
von D. G. Frisoni).

The influence
of Roman Baroque
(Bernini, Borromini)
north of the Alps.
Left: *Salzburg.*
Collegiate church
(J. B. Fischer von Erlach,
1696).
Right: *Weingarten, Swabia.*
West front of the convent
church (C. Moosbrugger, 1715;
façade: with D. G. Frisoni).

121   Schneiders

Schneiders

Schneiders

Melk. Klosterkirche, Hauptschiffswand (Jacob Prandtauer, 1702—36).
Durchgehender Wellenrhythmus der reich profilierten Gesimse.

Melk. Nave wall (Jacob Prandtauer, 1702—36).
A wave-like rhythm flows through
the elaborately profiled cornice.

Weingarten. Kapitelle der Südwand im Mittelschiff (1715—24).
Monumentale Ruhe: Jeder der mächtigen Pfeiler mit vielstufigen Gesimsen
bleibt hier klar vom nächsten gesondert.

Weingarten. Nave capitals (1715—24).
Monumentality and isolation: each pier supports its own cornice.

123

Schmidt-Glassner

Links: *Würzburg*.
Residenz, Hofkirche
(Balthasar Neumann;
1733 gewölbt).
Geschmeidig umfaßt
der obere Umgang
die kleine Kapelle.

Left: *Würzburg*.
Residenz, Hofkirche
(Balthasar Neumann).
Completed 1733.

Rechts: *Valencia*. Kathedrale.
Westfront (K. Rudolf
und F. Vergara, 1703).
In stürmisch vor- und
zurückflutender Bewegung
preßt sich die Fassade
zwischen die angrenzenden
Gebäude.

Right: *Valencia*. Cathedral.
The west front (K. Rudolf
and F. Vergara, 1703).
In dramatic movement,
the façade presses forward
between the adjoining
buildings.

125   MAS

Aufsberg

In den Kirchen
der Brüder Asam
wird der Hochaltar
zur Mysterienbühne.
Im Dämmerlicht
schmaler Chöre vor hell
strahlenden Hintergründen
die heiligen Gestalten.
Links:
Weltenburg a. d. Donau.
Klosterkirche. St. Georg
mit dem Drachen und der
Königstochter (beg. 1717).
Rechts: *München.*
Johann-Nepomuk-Kirche
("Asamkirche"; beg. 1733).
Die Dreifaltigkeit.

In the churches
of the Asam brothers,
the High Altar becomes
the stage of a mystery play.
From the twilight
of the narrow choir,
sacred figures stand
out against a brilliantly
lit background.
Left: *Weltenburg, Bavaria.*
Convent church. St. George
and the dragon with the
princess (begun 1717).
Right: *Munich.*
Johann-Nepomuk-Kirche
("Asam church", beg. 1733).
The Holy Trinity.

127   Neumeister

Wolynski

Jeiter

Rom. S. Croce in Gerusalemme (Gregorini und Passalacqua, beg. 1743). Späteste Phase des römischen Barock.
Im Schwung der gegeneinanderspielenden Teile: ein Dokument des „Rokoko".

Rome. S. Croce in Gerusalemme (D. Gregorini and P. Passalacqua, begun 1743).
In the interplay of all its parts a typical Rococo façade.

130

Jeiter

Rom. S. Giovanni in Laterano (A. Galilei, 1735).
Hier wird, in blockhafter Ruhe, der im Barock latente „Klassizismus" sichtbar.

Rome. S. Giovanni in Laterano (A. Galilei, 1735).
In this example of Late Roman Baroque: the calm and the block-like solidity of the coming "Classic" revival.

131

Weber

Jeiter

Stockholm. Riddarholmskirche. Kapelle Karls XII.
(Tessin d. Ä. 1671 beg.; beendet von C. Harleman, 1743).
Die achteckige Kapelle zählt zu den wenigen plastisch empfundenen Bauwerken
des schwedischen Barock.

Stockholm. Riddarholms church. Chapel of King Charles XII
(begun 1671 by N. Tessin the Elder, completed by C. Harleman, 1743).
The octagonal chapel is of a plasticity of form rarely found
in Swedish Baroque architecture.

Wiblingen, Oberschwaben. Klosterkirche, Fassade
(J. M. Fischer und J. G. Specht, 1750–1783).
Plastische Kraft des Barock, doch ernste Glattflächigkeit
als Vorbote des Klassizismus. Schmuck nur noch am Portal.

Wiblingen, Swabia. Convent church, façade
(J. M. Fischer and J. G. Specht, 1750–1783). Great plasticity, though with its plain
and severe façade already a forerunner of the "Classic" revival.
No decoration except for the central doorway.

In weiträumigen Sälen gipfeln die prunkvollen Raumfolgen der Klöster. Oben: *Metten, Niederbayern.* Bibliothek des Klosters (F. J. Holzinger, 1706—20).
Rechts: *Salem, Bodensee.* Kaisersaal der ehem. Zisterzienserabtei (Stuck von Jos. Anton Feuchtmayer, 1708—10).

Spaciousness and splendour in Baroque monasteries. Above: *Metten, Bavaria.* The library (F. J. Holzinger, 1706—20).
Right: *Salem, Lake Constance.* Kaisersaal ("Emperor's hall") of the former Cistercian abbey (plasterwork by Jos. Anton Feuchtmayer, 1708—10).

134

Schneiders

Schneiders

In den Bibliotheken wird die praktische Aufgabe zu großartig-glanzvollen oder auch liebenswürdig-intimen Lösungen geführt.
Links: *Wien*. Nationalbibliothek in der Hofburg (Entw. J. Bernh. Fischer v. Erlach; erb. v. Jos. Em. Fischer v. Erlach, 1722—37).
Oben: *Schussenried, Württemberg*. Bibliothek (Dom. Zimmermann, 1754—61).

Function, magnificently ennobled. Left: *Vienna*. Nationalbibliothek in the Hofburg (the former Imperial Palace).
(Designed by J. Bernh. Fischer von Erlach, built by Jos. Em. Fischer von Erlach; 1722—37).
Above: *Schussenried, Württemberg*. The library (Dom. Zimmermann, 1754—61).

Kersting

Coimbra, Portugal. Universitätsbibliothek (J. F. Ludwig, 1717–23).
Palastartig öffnen sich axiale Raumfluchten in hohen Arkaden.

Coimbra, Portugal. University library (J. F. Ludwig, 1717–23).
A palatial arrangement of tall rooms along a central axis.

Cadiz, Andalusien. Kathedrale. Blick in den Chor (Vicente Acero, 1722).
Im Bildzentrum der überkuppelte Altarraum und die kurvierten Vierungspfeiler.

Cadiz, Andalusia. Cathedral.
View into the choir (Vicente Acero, 1722).

Vierzehnheiligen, Franken.
Links: Feingliedrig,
in elastischer Bewegung,
erhebt sich die Wallfahrtskirche über dem Maintal.
(Balthasar Neumann,
seit 1743).
Rechts: Um den Gnadenaltar
als Mitte schwingt
der gesamte Bau,
der drei ovale Räume
mit kurvierenden Seiten-
schiffen verschmilzt.

Vierzehnheiligen, Franconia.
Left: the pilgrimage church
(Balthasar Neumann,
begun 1743), rising above
the Main valley.
Right: the whole interior,
formed of three ovals
and curving aisles,
streams round the altar
of the Fourteen Saints
at the centre.

Jeiter   **140**

Geschwungene Kapitelle – in Stein wie Stuck oder als illusionistische Architekturmalerei – sind Teil der Dynamik,
die den gesamten Baukörper ergreift. Links: *Vierzehnheiligen*. Kapitell (B. Neumann, 1743).
Oben: *Birnau, Bodensee.* Klosterkirche. Ausschnitt aus dem Fresko mit dem Engelskonzert (G. B. Götz, 1749).

Curvilinear capitals, whether in stone, stucco or as part of *trompe-l'œil*, are but one aspect of Baroque dynamism.
Left: *Vierzehnheiligen*. Capital (Balthasar Neumann, 1743).
Above: *Birnau, Lake Constance*. Convent church. Detail from the Angels' Concert (G. B. Götz, 1749).

Ruhig-klare Gliederung, überspielt von verschwenderisch blühender Dekoration, in den Kirchen Johann Michael Fischers.
Oben: *Ottobeuren, Oberschwaben*. Klosterkirche (1737–66; Stuck von J. M. Feichtmayr).
Rechts: *Zwiefalten, Oberschwaben*. Klosterkirche (1740–65; Stuck von Joh. Mich. Feichtmayr seit 1747).

Two churches by Johann Michael Fischer. Calm and clear articulation, with lavishly decorated interiors.
Above: *Ottobeuren, Swabia*. Convent church (1737–66; plasterwork by J. M. Feichtmayr).
Right: *Zwiefalten, Swabia*. Convent church (1740–65; the plasterwork by Joh. Mich. Feichtmayr, begun 1747).

144

Kirche „in der Wies" bei Steingaden, Oberbayern. (Dom. und Joh. Bapt. Zimmermann, 1745—54). Schlicht das Äußere (links), überraschend farbig und reich das Innere (rechts), ein Kleinod aus der spätesten Sonderentwicklung des sakralen Barock in Deutschland.

Steingaden, Bavaria. The pilgrimage church In der Wies ("on the meadow"). By Dominikus and Johann Baptist Zimmermann, 1745—54. The plain and unadorned façade (left) contrasts with the rich interior (right), one of the jewels of the last phase of German Baroque

147

Mehrschichtigkeit der Wandabschlüsse und sensibel gestaltete Fenster verleihen den Wallfahrtskirchen des Dominikus Zimmermann heitere Leichtigkeit. Oben: *Steinhausen, Oberschwaben* (1728–33). Rechts: *Kirche in der Wies.* Blick auf die Oberwand des Chors.

The gradual transition from walls to ceiling and judiciously placed windows make the interiors of Dominikus Zimmermann's pilgrimage churches appear light and gay. Above: *Steinhausen, Swabia* (1728–33). Right: the church *In der Wies.* View towards the choir.

148

E. Müller

Wagner

Wilhering, Oberösterreich. Klosterkirche. Im vielfach aufgebrochenen Rahmen der stuckierten Wölbung das große Deckenfresko „Triumph der Kirche". (B. Altomonte, nach 1733).

Wilhering, Austria. Convent church.
The elaborate plaster ceiling with the fresco "Triumph of the Church". (B. Altomonte, after 1733).

Neresheim, Württemberg. Klosterkirche (1747—92). Das letzte Werk Balthasar Neumanns. Aus der rational errechneten Durchdringung ovaler Räume entsteht ein organisches, lichtes Gebilde von kathedralen Ausmaßen.

Neresheim, Württemberg. Convent church (1747—92). Balthasar Neumann's last work. The church of the dimensions of a cathedral, is a brilliant example of its architect's great gift for carefully worked-out mathematical composition.

Schmidt-Glassner

Links: *Einsiedeln, Schweiz.*
Klosterkirche (C. Moos-
brugger, Brüder Asam,
F. Kraus; 1719–50). Blick aus
dem Langhaus zum Chor.
Selbst das perspektivische
Gitter dient dem Eindruck
des Ineinanderfließens
der Raumteile.
Rechts: *St. Gallen, Schweiz.*
Stiftskirche (P. Thumb und
J. M. Beer, 1752–66). Der
viergeschossige Ostbau
enthält den Mönchschor.

Left: *Einsiedeln, Switzerland.* Convent church
(C. Moosbrugger, the
Asam brothers, and
F. Kraus, 1719–50). View
into the choir from the
nave. Even the perspective
design of the iron grilles
serves to enhance the
impression of uninterrupted
movement throughout the
building.
Right: *St. Gallen, Switzerland.* Convent church
(P. Thumb and J. M. Beer,
1752–66). The four-storied
eastern portion contains
the monks' choir.

153   Schneiders

Jeiter

Hamacher

Virtuose Leistungen barocker Handwerkskunst des 18. Jh. sind die schmiedeeisernen Gitter — mit sprießendem Rankenwerk und illusionistischer Perspektive. Oben: *Zwiefalten*. Klosterkirche. Rechts: *Kreuzlingen, Schweiz*. Klosterkirche.

Wrought-iron grilles with sprouting plant forms and illusionist perspective are amongst the finest achievements of the eighteenth-century Baroque craftsman. Above: *Zwiefalten, Swabia*. Convent church. Right: *Kreuzlingen, Switzerland*. Convent church.

154

Brühl bei Köln. Oberes Treppenhaus des Schlosses (Balthasar Neumann, 1744–65).

Schloss Brühl near Cologne. Staircase gallery (Balthasar Neumann, 1744–65).

Jeiter

Birnau, Bodensee. Stiftskirche (P. Thumb, 1746–50; Ausstattung J. A. Feuchtmayer und G. B. Götz).
Birnau, Lake Constance. Convent church (P. Thumb, 1746–50; painting and sculpture by J. A. Feuchtmayer and G. B. Götz).

Hamacher

Dem Daseinsgefühl der Zeit entsprechend, gewinnt der Schmuck selbst der Altäre sinnenfreudiges Leben — mit Putten als Verkörperung religiöser Allegorien. Links: *Birnau*. Vom Altarbaldachin (J. A. Feuchtmayer, um 1750). Oben: *Straubing, Niederbayern*. Ursulerinnenkirche. Putto vom Hochaltar (E. Q. Asam, beg. 1736).

Baroque gaiety and exuberance even extends to the decoration of the Altar, with putti as vehicles of religious allegory. Left: *Birnau*. From the baldacchino (J. A. Feuchtmayer, c. 1750). Above: *Straubing, Bavaria*. Church of the Ursulines. Putto from the High Altar (E. Q. Asam, begun 1736).

159

Kunstvoll skulptiertes Gestühl – ein wesentlicher Teil spätbarocker Raumgestaltung.
Oben: *Cordoba, Andalusien*. Kathedrale, Chorgestühl (P. D. Cornejo, 1748–57).
Rechts: *Ottobeuren*. Klosterkirche. Südorgel, verbunden mit Chorgestühl (Jos. Christian, 1755–64).

Elaborately carved choir stalls, an important feature of the Late Baroque interior.
Above: *Cordova, Andalusia*. Cathedral, choir stalls (P. D. Cornejo, 1748–57).
Right: *Ottobeuren*. Convent church. The south organ, with choir stalls below (Jos. Christian, 1755–64).

Baur

Schmauss-Bavaria

Der großen Bedeutung entsprechend, die der Musik im 18. Jh. zufällt, werden die Orgeln mit liebevoller Sorgfalt in den Gesamtschmuck einbezogen.
Links: *Ochsenhausen, Oberschwaben*. Stiftskirche; Aufgang zur großen Orgel von Josef Gabler (1725—30).
Oben: *Wilhering, Oberösterreich*. Klosterkirche (beg. 1733). Seitenorgel über dem Chorgestühl (Dekoration J. G. Üblher).

163 Baroque organs as part of the general design. Left: *Ochsenhausen, Swabia*. Convent church. The steps to the great organ (1725—30).
Above: *Wilhering, Austria*. Convent church (begun 1733). One of the smaller organs above the choir stalls (decoration by J. G. Üblher).

Mittelalterliche Kirchen wurden im 18. Jh. vielfach barock umgestaltet.
Oben: *Kloster Neustift, Südtirol.* Blick aus dem Chor auf Mittelschiff und nördliches Seitenschiff (Weihe 1198; Barockisierung 1734–37).
Rechts: *Rottenbuch, Oberbayern.* Pfarrkirche. (Spätgotischer Umbau einer romanischen Kirche; Barockisierung 1737–42.)

Medieval churches were frequently re-modelled in the eighteenth century. Above: *Neustift Convent, South Tyrol.*
View from the choir into the nave and the north transept (consecrated 1198, re-modelled 1734–37).
Right: *Rottenbuch, Bavaria.* Parish church (a Romanesque church re-modelled during the Late Gothic and again during the Baroque, 1737–42).

Brieg, Schlesien. Pfarrkirche (1746). Der um gekurvte Emporen und Pfeiler flutende Raum mündet in einer virtuos illusionistisch auf den flachen Grund gemalten Architektur.

Brieg, Silesia. Parish church (1746). A vista of curving galleries and piers, terminating in *trompe-l'œil.*

166

Kobylko, Polen. Pfarrkirche (Longhi und Fontana, 1741–63). Die Malerei über dem Hochaltar leitet unmerklich
zur Halbkuppel über, die sich in den Himmel zu öffnen scheint.

Kobylko, Poland. Parish church (Longhi and Fontana, 1741–63). Almost imperceptibly, the frescos above the High Altar
guide the eye into the vaulted hemisphere, which seems to open to the sky.

167

Burghley House, Northamptonshire.
"The Heaven Room" (Wandmalerei von
Verrio, 1700). Die Wände verwandeln sich in offene Säulenhallen.
Die Grenzen zwischen Schein und Wirklichkeit werden verwischt.

Burghley House, Northamptonshire.
"The Heaven Room" (frescos by
Verrio, 1700). The walls are transformed into open arcaded halls.
Physical reality and illusion become one.

Madrid. Königliches Schloß. Gasparini-Zimmer (Girardini, nach 1738).
Am Ende der Epoche steht nicht mehr die Sehnsucht nach dem Götterhimmel,
sondern nach der Natur. Mit Motiven aus den Tropen und dem Fernen
Osten werden hier die Wände in eine Laubenarchitektur aufgelöst.

Madrid. Royal palace. Gasparini room (Girardini, 1738). The end of an epoch:
the accent is now on the beauties of Nature rather than the glories of the
next world. The walls are transformed into a bower by a luxuriance
of tropical and oriental motifs.

168

Alinari

Ullstein

Wallfahrtskirchen in beherrschender Höhe. Der Wildheit der Natur tritt die ordnende Gewalt des Schöpfers, symbolisiert in seinem Heiligtum, gegenüber. Oben: *Madonna di S. Luca bei Bologna* (C. Dotti, 1723–37). Unten: *Basilica Superga bei Turin* (F. Juvara, 1717–31). Die glanzvollste Bergkirche des Barock.

Pilgrimage churches in a mountain setting, as symbols of the Creator's might amidst the wildness of Nature. Above: *Madonna di S. Luca near Bologna* (C. Dotti, 1723–37). Below: *the Superga, near Turin* (Filippo Juvara, 1717–31), the most magnificent of all the Baroque mountain churches.

170

Gassilow

Dubrowizy bei Moskau. Kirche Mariä Erscheinung (1690–1704; Architekt unbek., Skulpturen Konrad Osner zugeschr.). Zentralbau aus vier Konchen mit oktogonalem Turm, reich mit Ornament und figürlicher Plastik geschmückt. Eines der originellsten Beispiele für die Übernahme barocker Formen.

Dubrovitsi, Russia. Church of the Virgin of the Sign (1690–1704; architect unknown, sculpture attributed to Konrad Osner). Centralised building on a quatrefoil plan, with octagonal tower, covered in sculpture. One of the most original interpretations of Baroque forms.

Die ornamentalen Gärten des Barock bilden den Übergang vom Menschenwerk der Architektur zur freien Landschaft.
Links: *Hannover. Schloß Herrenhausen. Park* (Charbonnier, um 1700; Vorkriegszustand). Oben: *Middachten bei De Steeg, Holland* (17. Jh.).
Umgebautes mittelalterliches Wasserschloß, in origineller Weise über den Graben hinweg von axial gerichteten Höfen und Gärten umgeben.

The ornamental gardens of the Baroque form the transition from Nature to the works of Man.
Left: *Hanover. Schloss Herrenhausen. The park* (laid out by Charbonnier, c. 1700; pre-war photograph).
Above: *Middachten near De Steeg, Holland* (17th cent.). A re-modelled medieval moated castle, surrounded by formal gardens.

Schneiders

YAN

H. Retzlaff

Das Lustschloß bildet mit seiner axial geordneten Parkanlage ein einheitliches Gesamtkunstwerk. Oben: *Wien*. Gartenpalast des Prinzen Eugen. Oberes Belvedere, Hofseite (Lucas von Hildebrandt, 1721). Unten: *Queluz, Portugal*. Sommerpalast (M. V. de Oliveira, um 1750). Gartenfront und Fontänen. Rechts: *Fulda*. Orangerie im Park des fürstäbtlichen Residenzschlosses (M. v. Welsch, 1721–30).

The palace and its formal gardens as components of one homogeneous work of art. Above: *Vienna*. The garden palace of Prince Eugene, Upper Belvedere. The entrance front (Lucas von Hildebrandt, 1721). Below: *Queluz, Portugal*. The summer palace (M. V. de Oliveira, c. 1750). Garden front and fountains. Right: *Fulda, Hesse*. The orangery in the park of the Residenz (M. von Welsch, 1721–30).

Hansa-Luftbild

Potsdam. Schloß Sanssouci (G. W. von Knobelsdorff, 1745—47).
Ein Landsitz, für Friedrich d. Gr. und seinen engsten
Freundeskreis erbaut.

Potsdam. Sanssouci (G. W. von Knobelsdorff, 1745—47).
A country seat built for Frederick the Great
and his intimate circle.

Wien. Schloß Schönbrunn (beg. v. J. B. Fischer v. Erlach 1696;
von Pacassi 1744—49 umgestaltet). Die kaiserliche Residenz —
zur Entfaltung eines großen höfischen Zeremoniells bestimmt.

Vienna. Schönbrunn Palace (begun by J. B. Fischer von Erlach 1696,
re-modelled by Pacassi 1744—49). The Imperial palace,
a splendid setting for the ceremonial of the Court.

In der Anlage von Treppen und Wasserspielen nach dem axialen System entfaltet der späte Barock theatralische Phantasie.
Oben: *Braga*, Portugal. Wallfahrtskirche Bom Jesus do Monte (Treppenanlage und Fassade, beg. 1723).
Rechts: *Kassel*. Schloß Wilhelmshöhe, Herkuleskaskade mit Riesenschloß (Guernieri, zwischen 1701 und 1718).

Elaborate axial systems of staircases and water gardens are amongst the finest expressions of Late Baroque fantasy.
Above: *Braga, Portugal*. The pilgrimage church of Bom Jesus do Monte (staircase and façade begun 1723).
Right: *Cassel*. Schloss Wilhelmshöhe. Hercules cascade with Riesenschloss ("giant's castle"). Built by Guernieri between 1701 and 1718.

Üppig und prunkvoll werden auch die Zweckbauten für die Wasserversorgung errichtet. Oben: *Stift Kremsmünster, Österreich* (Carlone, 1690–92).
Säulenhallen umschließen die Fischbassins für die Fastenküche. Rechts: *Rom*. Fontana Trevi (N. Salvi, 1762).

Even purely functional structures serving the water supply share in the splendour of churches and palaces. Above: *Kremsmünster, Austria* (Carlone, 1690–92).
Pillared halls surround the fish tanks for the kitchens. Right: *Rome*. Fontana Trevi (N. Salvi, 1762).

180

Ullstein

Großzügige Wasserspiele und intime Pavillons — charakteristische Bestandteile barocker Parkanlagen.
Links: *Potsdam*. Sanssouci, Chinesisches Haus (J. G. Büring, 1754). Wohl die reizvollste Chinoiserie in einem europäischen Barockgarten.
Oben: *Caserta bei Neapel*. Königliches Schloß (Vanvitelli, 1752—74). Diana-Brunnen.

Extensive water gardens and small, intimate pavilions are an integral part of many Baroque palaces.
Left: *Potsdam*. Sanssouci, the "Chinesisches Haus" (Chinese House) by J. G. Büring, 1754. Probably the most delightful piece of Chinoiserie
in a European Baroque garden. Above: *Caserta, near Naples*. Royal Palace (Vanvitelli, 1752—74). The Fountain of Diana in the park.

Vorliebe des Barock für Wasseranlagen zur Belebung der Gartenarchitektur.
Oben: *Leningrad.* Schloß Peterhof (Le Blond, beg. 1715). Der von Fontänen begleitete Kanal führt zum Meer.
Rechts oben: *Villa Pisani bei Strà, unweit Venedig* (Frigimelica und Preti; 1735—56). Der Kanal, auf den Mittelrisalit der Gartenfassade bezogen, endet
in dem breit geschwungenen Bassin. Unten: *Settignano bei Florenz.* Villa Gamberaia (nach 1750). Schon im flächigeren Stil des beginnenden Klassizismus.

The Baroque love of water gardens. Above: *Leningrad.* Peterhof (Le Blond; begun 1715). The canal, flanked by fountains, leads into the sea.
Right, above: *Strà, near Venice* (Frigimelica and Preti; 1735—56). Villa Pisani. The canal terminates in a pool with curving sides.
Below: *Settignano, near Florence.* Villa Gamberaia (post 1750). The flatter style of the dawn of the Classic Revival.

184

R. Müller

Links oben: *Schloß Zarskoje Selo b. Leningrad* (beg. 1743; Rastrelli ab 1747).
Die immensen Komplexe der Zarenschlösser vereinigen die Erfahrungen ganz Europas im Palastbau.
Unten: *Harewood House, Yorkshire* (Robert Adam, um 1760).
Anklänge an Palladio, barock das Pavillonsystem.

Left, above: *Tsarskoe Selo, near Leningrad* (begun 1743, completed by Rastrelli 1747).
The vast buildings of the Imperial Russian court mirror the entire history of the European Baroque palace.
Below: *Harewood House, Yorkshire* (Robert Adam, c. 1760).
Vaguely Palladian, with Baroque pavilions.

British Travel and Holiday Ass.

Eremitage bei Bayreuth.
Wasserspiele (um 1750).
Grottenarchitektur gehört zur Naturtändelei
der Epoche.

The Hermitage, near Bayreuth.
Water displays (c. 1750). Grottos
as an expression of the Baroque fondness
for toying with "natural" effects.

Das Pavillon-System gab die Möglichkeit zu reicher und festlicher Gliederung großangelegter Architekturen.
Oben: *Dresden*. Zwinger, Wallpavillon (Pöppelmann, ab 1711). Steinarchitektur als Rahmen für höfische Feste.
Rechts: *Würzburg*. Residenz, Gartenfront (Balthasar Neumann, beg. 1735).

The architecture of pleasure. Above: *Dresden*. The Zwinger. Wall pavilion (Pöppelmann, begun 1711).
Right: *Würzburg*. The Residenz. Garden front (Balthasar Neumann, begun 1735).

Die Treppenhäuser der Schlösser entwickeln sich, besonders in Deutschland, zu prunkvollen Eigengebilden.
Oben: *Schloß Weißenstein bei Pommersfelden, Franken* (Joh. Dientzenhofer und L. v. Hildebrandt, 1711–16).
Rechts: *Würzburg*. Residenz. Die krönende Leistung unter den Treppenbauten Balthasar Neumanns (seit 1737).

In Germany, in particular, staircases tend to become magnificent structures of their own.
Above: *Weissenstein near Pommersfelden, Franconia* (Joh. Dientzenhofer and Lucas von Hildebrandt, 1711–16).
Right: *Würzburg*. The Residenz. The finest of Balthasar Neumann's staircases (begun 1737).

190

Würzburg. Residenz. Kaisersaal (Balth. Neumann, 1737;
Fresken von Tiepolo, 1752). Der Saal erscheint von beinahe zerbrechlicher Zartheit
und wohlig in die Horizontale gebreitet.

Würzburg. The Residenz. Kaisersaal ("Emperor's Hall"). By Balth. Neumann, 1737;
frescos by Tiepolo, 1752. A room of comfortably horizontal emphasis,
with decoration of an almost fragile delicacy.

Stupinigi bei Turin. Der ovale Zentralraum
des gewaltigen Jagdschlosses (Juvara, 1729–31) zeigt energische Vertikaltendenz.

Turin. Palazzo Stupinigi (Filippo Juvara, 1729–31).
The Great Saloon shows a strong vertical emphasis.

Palastbauten in Italien. Links oben: *Rom*. Palazzo Doria. Spiegelgalerie (Vanvitelli, nach 1734).
Unten: *Caserta bei Neapel*. Der Palazzo Reale (Vanvitelli, beg. 1752) enthält das größte Treppenhaus Italiens.
Oben: *Caserta*. Vom achteckigen Kuppelraum — als Endpunkt der Treppe — eröffnen sich weite Raumfluchten.

Italian palaces. Left, above: *Rome*. Palazzo Doria, the gallery of mirrors (Vanvitelli, begun 1734).
Below: *Caserta, near Naples*. The Palazzo Reale (L. Vanvitelli, 1752), with Italy's most monumental staircase.
Above: *Caserta*. The octagonal domed hall as the termination of the staircase, opens into splendid vistas.

Venedig. Palazzo Labia, Fresko im großen Salon: Antonius und Kleopatra (G. B. Tiepolo, um 1745–50).
Echte Architektur geht unmerklich in Malerei über.

Venice. Palazzo Labia. Fresco in the great saloon: Antony and Cleopatra (G. B. Tiepolo, c. 1745–50).
Architecture merges almost imperceptibly into *trompe-l'œil.*

Mortirone bei Brescia. Villa Lecchi, Ballsaal (Fresken von Lecchi und Carlini, 1745). Das Verschränken und Verschmelzen der Räume, eines der Hauptprinzipien barocker Baukunst, spricht sich in der gemalten Scheinarchitektur überzeugend aus.

Mortirone, near Brescia. Villa Lecchi, ball-room (frescos by Lecchi and Carlini, 1745). The impression of continuous movement, one of the basic principles of Baroque architecture, assisted by *trompe-l'œil.*

Neumeister

Hamacher

Das heroische Pathos der Freskomalerei löst sich im spätesten Barock zu bukolischer Tändelei.
Links: *Schloß Leitheim bei Donauwörth*. Deckenmalerei, Ausschnitt (G. B. Götz, 1751). Oben: *München*, Schloß Nymphenburg, Steinerner Saal.
Die Fresken von Joh. Bapt. Zimmermann (1756) verschmelzen mit der Stuckdekoration.

Late Baroque fresco painting. Heroic pathos yields to bucolic playfulness.
Left: *Schloss Leitheim, near Donauwörth*. Ceiling fresco, detail (G. B. Götz, 1751). Above: *Munich*. Schloss Nymphenburg. Great Hall.
The frescos (Johann Baptist Zimmermann, 1756) merge with the plasterwork.

Granada. Santa Cruz la Real, jetzt Santa Escolastica. Kapelle der Virgen del Rosaria (1726–73).
In die phantastische Dekoration, die Wände und Kuppel gänzlich ausfüllt, sind unzählige Spiegel eingelassen.

Granada. Santa Cruz la Real, now Santa Escolastica. The Rosary Chapel (1726–73).
Mirrors everywhere, set amidst phantastic decoration which covers walls and ceiling.

MAS

Valencia. Portal am Palast des Marques de Dos Aguas (1740—44; Entw. Hipolito Rovira, Ausf. Ignacio Vergara).
Menschliche Körper und tropisch wucherndes Pflanzenwerk sind kaum mehr voneinander zu lösen.

Valencia. The palace of the Marques de Dos Aguas (1740—44 by Ignacio Vergara, based on the designs of Hipolito Rovira).
Human forms and luxuriating vegetation are almost inextricably bound up.

Neumeister

Die luxuriöse Welt des höfischen Lebens
spielt mit Elementen der „unverfälschten" Natur.
Oben: *Mantua*. Palazzo Ducale. Refektorium (Anselmi, um 1776)
mit einer Grotte und gemalter Gartendekoration.
Unten: *Pommersfelden*. Muschelsaal (1711–16).

"Unspoilt nature" as the diversion of sophisticated eighteenth-century courts.
Above: *Mantua*. Palazzo Ducale. The refectory (Anselmi, c. 1776)
with grotto and painted garden decoration.
Below: *Pommersfelden, Franconia*. Muschelsaal ("hall of shells"), 1711–16.

München. Schloß Nymphenburg. Steinerner Saal
(Effner, 1715; F. Cuvilliés d. Ä. 1756–57; Dekoration J. B. Zimmermann).
Würdevoller Zusammenklang der großen Pilastergliederung
mit Stukkaturen und Deckenfresko.

Munich. Schloss Nymphenburg.
The Great Hall (J. Effner, 1715, and F. Cuvilliés the Elder, 1756–57;
decoration by J. B. Zimmermann).
Pilasters, plasterwork and ceiling fresco form
a harmonious and dignified whole.

Abstraktes Ornament und illusionistisches Naturbild, mit vollendeter Leichtigkeit und Eleganz entworfen und ausgeführt, schmücken die schönsten Räume des deutschen Rokoko. Links: *München*. Nymphenburg, Jagdschlößchen Amalienburg. Spiegelsaal (F. Cuvilliés d. Ä., beg. 1734; Stuck von J. B. Zimmermann, Schnitzereien von J. Dietrich). Oben: *München*. Residenz, „Reiche Zimmer", Schlafzimmer (Cuvilliés, nach 1729; Vorkriegsaufnahme).

A mixture of abstract ornament and *trompe-l'œil*, designed with the utmost elegance and virtuosity, is characteristic of many of the finest German Rococo interiors. Left: *Munich*. Nymphenburg, Amalienburg. Spiegelsaal ("Hall of Mirrors"; by F. Cuvilliés the Elder, begun 1734, plasterwork by J. B. Zimmermann, carvings by J. Dietrich). Above: *Munich*. Residenz, "Reiche Zimmer". Bedroom (F. Cuvilliés, after 1729; pre-war photograph).

205

Baur

Potsdam. Sanssouci, Marmorsaal (G. W. von Knobelsdorff, 1746). Das Gegengewicht zu den majestätischen Säulengruppen im ovalen Speisesaal wird durch zarten Dekor erreicht, der Kuppelgesims, Türen und Fußboden überspielt.

Potsdam. Sanssouci. Marmorsaal ("Marble Hall"; G. W. von Knobelsdorff, 1746).
The effect of the heavy columns is balanced by the light and delicate decoration which spreads over cornice, doors and floor.

Baur

Potsdam. Stadtschloß, Kolonnaden und Mittelrisalit (Knobelsdorff, 1744–51).
Die Bauten von Potsdam prägen das französische Vorbild und den Geist der römischen Antike in eine spezifisch friderizianische Form um.

Potsdam. The royal palace. Centre block and colonnades (G. W. von Knobelsdorff, 1744–51). The buildings of Potsdam are a specifically Prussian interpretation of French eighteenth-century models in a manner reminiscent of Classic Rome.

Claydon House, Buckinghamshire. Nordhalle, Chinoiserien (Lightfoot, 1752—68).
Frei bewegtes Chinoiserie-Rocaille-Ornament, dazu streng dorisierender Fries.

Claydon House, Buckinghamshire. Entrance hall (the only known work of a carpenter-contractor referred to as Mr. Lightfoot, 1752—68).
The freedom of the chinoiserie rocaille ornament contrasts with the severe Doric frieze.

Baur

Potsdam. Stadtschloß, Schlafzimmer (Dekoration J. A. Nahl, 1744–51).
Heiter sprießendes asymmetrisches Rankenwerk rahmt die Spiegel.

Potsdam. The royal palace. Bedroom (decoration by J. A. Nahl, 1744–51).
Mirrors set amidst freely flowing asymmetric forms.

Birzele-Bavaria

Spiegel täuschen unendliche Zimmerfluchten vor und erhöhen die schimmernde Pracht der Ausstattung.
Oben: *Augsburg*. Schaezler-Palais, Festsaal, im Wandspiegel gesehen (1765—70). Rechts: *Ansbach*. Residenz, Spiegelkabinett (1738—44).

Mirrors create the illusion of long vistas and add to the general splendour. Above: *Augsburg*. Schaezler-Palais. The ball-room, seen through a mirror (1765—70).
Right: *Ansbach*, Bavaria. Residenz. The Spiegelkabinett ("Cabinet of Mirrors"), 1738—44.

Busch

E. Müller

Gundermann

Das Logentheater — eine neue Aufgabe für den Architekten — entspricht der im Rang genau abgestuften Hofgesellschaft.
Versailles. Opéra Royale, obere Ränge des Zuschauerraumes (A. J. Gabriel, 1748—63).
Bayreuth. Zuschauerraum des Theaters (J. Saint-Pierre, 1744; Dekoration G. u. C. Bibiena).

The tiered auditorium of the Baroque theatre, a new task for the architect, corresponds to the rigid system of precedence of the Baroque Court.
Versailles. Opéra Royale. The gallery (A. J. Gabriel, 1748—63).
Bayreuth. The auditorium of the theatre (J. Saint-Pierre, 1744; decoration by G. and C. Bibiena).

Nancy, Lothringen. Place Royale. Ausdruck des französischen Rokoko: Platzanlage und Architektur gleiten geschmeidig ineinander über und verbinden sich mit kunstvoll gerahmten Gartenanlagen und Fontänen.
Links: Palais du Gouvernement (G. Boffrand 1715; beendet von Héré de Corny, 1753–55). Oben: Fontaine de Neptune (Lamour, 1760).

Nancy. Place Royale. One of the finest expressions of French Rococo. A harmonious composition of buildings, gardens and fountains.
Left: Palais du Gouvernement (G. Boffrand, 1715; completed by Héré de Corny, 1753–55).
Above: Fontaine de Neptune (by Lamour, 1760).

Patrizierhäuser schmücken sich im 17. Jh. mit schweren Girlanden und Gehängen nach oberitalienischem Muster, wohl durch Holland vermittelt.
Im 18. Jh. überzieht feinteiliges Rocaillewerk die Fassade. Oben: *Thorn*. Haus Dambski (1693). Rechts: *Innsbruck*. Helblinghaus (um 1730 barockisiert).

Many patrician town houses are decorated with swags and garlands in the 17th century, with rocaille work in the 18th century.
Above: *Torun*. Dambski House (1693). Right: *Innsbruck*. Helblinghaus (façade re-modelled c. 1730).

216

Defner

217

Aufsberg

Storz

Die Stuckdekoration wandelt sich von üppiger Fülle zu zartestem asymmetrischem Formenspiel.
Links: *Ellwangen, Württemberg.* Wallfahrtskirche auf dem Schönenberg. Stuckdecke (Heinrich Mayer, 1685).
Oben: *Salem, Bodensee.* Stuckdetail (J. G. Dirr, 1765) im Abts-Salon des ehem. Zisterzienserklosters.

Plasterwork from exuberant opulence to delicate asymmetry.
Left: *Ellwangen, Württemberg.* Pilgrimage church on the Schönenberg. Ceiling (Heinrich Mayer, 1685).
Above: *Salem, Lake Constance.* Detail (J. G. Dirr, 1765) from the Abbot's room in the former Cistercian monastery.

219

R. Müller

Jauer, Schlesien. Friedenskirche (um 1650—55).
Mehrgeschossige Emporen als charakteristisches
Merkmal protestantischer Kirchen.

Der protestantische Kirchenbau zeigt schon früh klassizistische Tendenzen,
der katholische erst gegen Ende des 18. Jh. Rechts oben: *Neresheim, Württemberg.* Orgel der Klosterkirche (1796).
Unten: *Bern, Schweiz.* Reformierte Heiliggeistkirche (Schildknecht, 1726—29).

Jauer, Silesia. Friedenskirche (c. 1650—55).
Galleries, a characteristic feature
of Protestant churches.

Classic trends, not evident in Catholic churches until the late eighteenth century, appear at a comparatively early
stage in Protestant church architecture. Above: *Neresheim, Württemberg.* The organ in the convent church (1796).
Below: *Berne, Switzerland.* The Protestant Heiliggeistkirche (N. Schildknecht, 1726—29).

Pragher

Hesse

Dresden. Frauenkirche (G. Bähr, 1726—38; kriegszerstört). Der energisch modellierte Bau
erhält seine geniale Prägung durch die harmonische Verschmelzung mit der glockenhaften Kuppel.

Dresden. Frauenkirche (G. Bähr, 1726—38, destroyed during the last war). One of the most magnificent examples of Protestant church architecture.

Dresden. Frauenkirche. Das Innere, ein überraschend zart akzentuierter Ovalraum,
von Emporen begleitet, schwingt dem szenisch gesteigerten Chor entgegen.

Dresden. Frauenkirche. Interior.

Eschen-Bavaria

Hamburg. St. Michaelis. Innenraum und Turm (Sonnin und Prey, 1751—61).
Zügige Kurvierung der Emporen (links) in der bedeutendsten evangelischen Kirche Norddeutschlands.
Abgerundete Kanten und betonte Gurtgesimse der oberen Turmgeschosse (oben) als Sockel des bekrönenden „Tempietto" (Sonnin, 1777—86).

Hamburg. St. Michaelis. Interior and tower (by Sonnin and Prey, 1751—61).
The most outstanding Protestant church building in Northern Germany. The top storey of the tower with its rounded edges
and heavy cornice is treated as the base of the surmounting "tempietto" (Sonnin, 1777—86).

London. St. John's,
Smith Square (Thomas Archer,
um 1720;
Inneres kriegszerstört).
Portico und dorisches Gesims
erinnern an die englische
Vorliebe für Palladio,
während in den Formen
der Türme
Borrominis Plastizität anklingt.

London. St. John's,
Smith Square (Thomas Archer,
c. 1720; the interior
was gutted during the last war).
Portico and Doric entablature
recall the English love
of Palladio, the towers
Borromini.

London. Christ Church,
Spitalfields. Turmfront
(N. Hawksmoor, 1723—29).
Mittelalterliche Elemente
verbinden sich
dem griechischen Vorbild.

London. Christ Church,
Spitalfields
(Nicholas Hawksmoor,
1723—29).
A combination of Greek
and medieval traits.

226

Stockholm. Schloß (N. Tessin d. J., 1690—1754).
Ein sparsam gegliederter Block
mit langen Fensterreihen —
römische Würde im Norden.

Stockholm. Royal Palace
(N. Tessin the Younger, 1690—1754).
Roman severity in the North:
an almost square block with long rows of windows.

Rechts oben: *Cambridge*. Senate House, Hauptfront (J. Gibbs u. Sir James Burrough, 1722—30).
Durch Säulen und Pilaster würdevoll und elegant konzentriert.
Unten: *Paris*. Hôtel de Soubise, Hauptfront (P. A. Delamaire, 1706—12).
Klassizistische Strenge, durch Rokokoplastik sparsam aufgelockert.

Right, above: *Cambridge*. Senate House. Principal façade (James Gibbs and Sir James Burrough, 1722—30).
An effect of compactness, accentuated by columns and pilasters.
Below: *Paris*. Hôtel de Soubise. Principal façade (P. A. Delamaire, 1706—12).
Classic severity, relieved by Rococo sculpture.

laender-
press

Jack
Scheer-
boom

Cash

Die Formenwelt des Barock, vorwiegend vermittelt durch italienische Architekten, durchdringt Polen und findet auch in Rußland Eingang.
Oben: *Leningrad*. Ehemal. Winterpalais, Mitteltrakt der Fassade (B. F. Rastrelli, 1754–62).
Rechts oben: *Schloß Wilanów b. Warschau*. (A. M. Locci, beg. 1681; Spazzio u. Fontana 1725–33).
Unten: *Leningrad:* Ehemal. Smolny-Kloster (Rastrelli, 1748 beg.). In der Mitte: „Kathedrale der Auferstehung".

Baroque in Russia and Poland. Above: *Leningrad*. The former Winter Palace (B. F. Rastrelli, 1754–62).
Right, above: the palace at *Wilanów near Warsaw* (begun by A. M. Locci, 1681; completed by Spazzio and Fontana, 1725–33).
Below: *Leningrad*. Former Smolny convent (begun by B. F. Rastrelli, 1748). Centre: Cathedral of the Resurrection.

In der 2. Hälfte des 18. Jh. kehrt die Architektur, zumal in Nordeuropa, mehr und mehr zu den von der Antike geprägten Grundformen zurück.
Der eigentliche Barockstil wird von akademischem Klassizismus abgelöst.
Oben: *Berlin*. Französischer Dom (K. v. Gontard, 1780). Rechts: *Paris*. Panthéon (J. G. Soufflot, Entw. 1755).

The second half of the eighteenth century, especially in Northern Europe,
is marked by a return to basic Classic forms. Baroque yields to the more academic Classic Revival.
Above: *Berlin*. Französischer Dom (K. von Gontard, 1780). Right: *Paris*: Panthéon (J. G. Soufflot, designed 1755).

234

Kerff

Göttingen. Treppenhaus in der ehem. Frauenklinik (Borheck, 1784).
In den kühl verhaltenen Formen
klingt barocker Schwung vernehmlich nach.

Göttingen. Staircase of the former women's hospital
(Borheck 1784). Cool and restrained forms,
still gently pulsating with Baroque movement.

Bremen. Detail von einem ehem. Patrizierhaus (um 1750;
heute in die Sparkasse eingebaut). Feinnerviges Dekor des norddeutschen Rokoko —
klassizistische Kühle einer noblen Fassade.

Bremen. Detail from the former town house of a patrician family
(c. 1750; now incorporated into the Sparkasse building).
The subtle elegance and Classic calm of North German Rococo.

Maré

Defner / Foto Marburg

Das Vorbild der Antike, in der Renaissance und latent auch im ganzen Barock wirkend, gewinnt die Oberhand.
Oben: *London*. Chiswick House. Die Galerie (Lord Burlington, beg. 1725). Rechts oben: *Schloß Schönbrunn bei Wien*. Gloriette (F. v. Hohenberg, voll. 1775).
Unten: *Schloß Maisons-Lafitte*. Vestibül (Mansart 1642–50; Dekoration Bélanger, 1779; Fontaine und Percier nach 1800).

The Classic spirit, active throughout the Renaissance and, indirectly, throughout the entire Baroque, re-asserts itself once more.
Above: *London*. Chiswick House. The gallery (Lord Burlington, begun 1725). Right, above: *Vienna*. Schönbrunn Palace. Gloriette (G. v. Hohenberg, compl. 1775).
Below: *Maisons-Lafitte, France*. The château. Entrance hall (F. Mansart, 1642–50, decoration by F. J. Bélanger, 1779, and after 1800 by P. F. L. Fontaine and Percier).

238

Windstosser

Schloß Wurzach, Allgäu. Eines der schönsten Treppenhäuser des ausklingenden Barock, entworfen von einem unbekannten Meister. (Nach 1750.)
Schloss Wurzach, Allgäu. One of the finest staircases of the last phase of the Baroque, by an unknown architect (after 1750).